That Elusive Extra Trick

If you were contemplating who, among the acknowledged bridge experts, would be the most likely to teach you some sharp tricks to raise your card play to a new plateau, you would undoubtedly think of Terence Reese and David Bird. This book proves the accuracy of your judgement.

In eight thought-provoking chapters, starting with the initial attack and winding up with advice on pressure play, you will find your perceptions and skill at the table being steadily enhanced by these redoubtable master players.

D1584926

That Elusive Extra Trick

Terence Reese & David Bird

For Catherine,
With very best wishes,

David Bird

VICTOR GOLLANCZ
in association with
PETER CRAWLEY

First published in Great Britain 1994
in association with Peter Crawley
by Victor Gollancz
A Division of the Cassell group
Villiers House, 41/47 Strand, London WC2N 5JE

A catalogue record for this book
is available from the British Library

ISBN 0 575 05816 1

Photoset in Great Britain by
Rowland Phototypesetting Ltd, Bury St Edmunds, Suffolk
and printed in Great Britain by St Edmundsbury Press Ltd,
Bury St Edmunds, Suffolk

Contents

Foreword

Most books on play describe standard forms of technique such as drawing trumps, finessing, setting up suits in dummy, that kind of thing. We have contributed our share of those. In this book we assume, for the most part, that the reader is familiar with the basic principles of play. We describe a variety of more advanced moves, the type that mark the difference between competent and expert play.

If you are already above average in your circle you will have no difficulty in understanding and, before long, executing all the forms of play that we describe.

1 *The First Attack*

Left-hand opponent leads, the dummy goes down, and you play . . .

Ah, but you must never play quickly at this point, even when dummy holds a singleton of the suit led. For a few tricks, at least, you have a distinct advantage over the defenders, because you can see 26 cards in partnership. At this stage you will be able to form a plan much more easily than they can.

In case you thought otherwise, you have every right to consider matters before you play from dummy. If right-hand opponent rudely plays a card before you have done so, treat it with disdain. One reason why you should always take your time is that there is no point in letting the opposition know whether the play is going to be easy or difficult.

The first three points you should consider will usually be:

(1) How many tricks are there on top or that can easily be established?

(2) Where do I go for the extra tricks that may be needed?

(3) Meanwhile, where does the danger lie? What is the worst they can do to me?

Let's look at a few deals where a hasty approach might lead you down a wrong path.

Play first on which suit?

On this first deal South is in 3NT and must decide which suit to attack first.

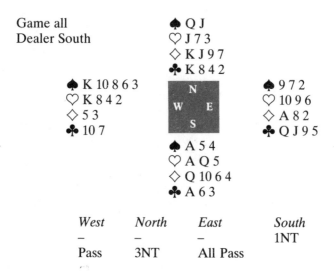

Game all ♠ Q J
Dealer South ♡ J 7 3
◇ K J 9 7
♣ K 8 4 2

♠ K 10 8 6 3
♡ K 8 4 2
◇ 5 3
♣ 10 7

♠ 9 7 2
♡ 10 9 6
◇ A 8 2
♣ Q J 9 5

♠ A 5 4
♡ A Q 5
◇ Q 10 6 4
♣ A 6 3

West	North	East	South
–	–	–	1NT
Pass	3NT	All Pass	

West leads ♣ 6 and dummy's jack holds the first trick. Since you can establish three tricks in diamonds and only one in either clubs or hearts, it may seem natural to play on diamonds first.

Let's see what will happen if you lead a low diamond from dummy at trick two. Since his partner has the long spades, East will rise with the ace of diamonds and lead a second spade.

Prospects will not be at all good after this start. Where did you go wrong? While you were taking your time at trick one, this is how you should have regarded the matter:

'I start with five top tricks; three more can be established in diamonds and one in hearts. Should I play on diamonds first or hearts? If East has the heart king, both lines will win. If West has the heart king and the diamond ace, both lines lose. In the remaining case West has the heart king, East the ace of diamonds. If I play on diamonds first East will win and clear the spades while West still has an entry, so it must be right to play on hearts first.'

In other words, you must attack the entry to the danger hand. When later you force out the other stopper, that opponent will have no entry to his partner's hand.

So, at trick two play a low heart to the queen. If West wins and returns the king of spades you will hold off and win the third round of spades. East will have no spade to return when you knock out the ace of diamonds.

On the next deal 3NT looked fairly secure and declarer gave the play no thought until it was too late.

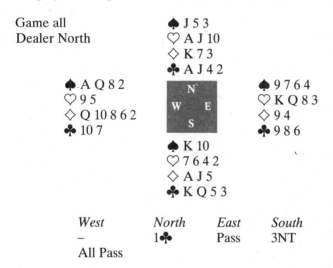

Game all — ♠ J 5 3
Dealer North — ♡ A J 10
♢ K 7 3
♣ A J 4 2

♠ A Q 8 2
♡ 9 5
♢ Q 10 8 6 2
♣ 10 7

♠ 9 7 6 4
♡ K Q 8 3
♢ 9 4
♣ 9 8 6

♠ K 10
♡ 7 6 4 2
♢ A J 5
♣ K Q 5 3

West	North	East	South
–	1♣	Pass	3NT
All Pass			

South was not one of the modern breed that considers the heart suit worth a mention. He bid a sensible 3NT and West's ♢ 6 lead ran to the 9 and jack. There was no hurry to play off the clubs (which might be useful for entry purposes), so declarer began with a heart to the 10, which lost to the queen. East returned a diamond and South won in hand with the ace. A second finesse in hearts was won by East's king. East led a spade to his partner's queen, and West played a third round of diamonds.

Not so good. A little belatedly, declarer paused to count the tricks in what at first had seemed an easy contract. He could see four clubs, three diamonds and the ace of hearts. Hoping his luck would turn, he cashed the ace of hearts. The suit failed to break, though, and a short while later West made the ace of spades and two more diamonds, putting the game one down.

Pity, because it wasn't really difficult to arrive at nine tricks. After the diamond lead declarer had eight on top. All he needed was a ninth in spades. He should have led the king of spades from hand at trick two.

Spotting the danger

Every suit is well guarded on the next deal and 3NT again seems a comfortable spot. There's danger lurking round the corner, though.

East–West game
Dealer South

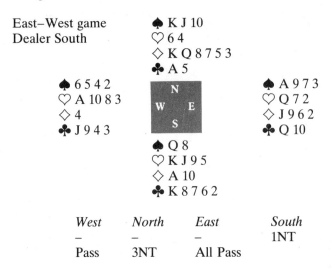

```
                    ♠ K J 10
                    ♡ 6 4
                    ◇ K Q 8 7 5 3
                    ♣ A 5
     ♠ 6 5 4 2         N           ♠ A 9 7 3
     ♡ A 10 8 3                    ♡ Q 7 2
     ◇ 4          W       E        ◇ J 9 6 2
     ♣ J 9 4 3        S            ♣ Q 10
                    ♠ Q 8
                    ♡ K J 9 5
                    ◇ A 10
                    ♣ K 8 7 6 2
```

West	North	East	South
–	–	–	1NT
Pass	3NT	All Pass	

Both the Qx in spades and A 10 in diamonds are good holdings in the declarer's hand, so you open an off-beat weak no-trump. West leads ♡ 3 against 3NT and you win East's queen with the king.

Suppose you play ace and another diamond now. You will then have to concede a diamond to East, the danger hand. He will play a second heart through, and if you play the 9 or jack West will cover. When you eventually play on spades East will win and play a third heart. That's one down, the defenders scoring three hearts, a diamond and a spade.

Whether West holds four or five hearts you won't mind losing a diamond trick to him. At trick two you should play a spade to the jack. East will probably win and play a heart to the 9 and 10. If West perseveres with hearts, that will give you a ninth trick. If, as is more likely, he switches, you will reach dummy with a spade and finesse ◇ 10. Even if the finesse loses, there is no damage that West can do to you.

Watch the entries

This is another hand where you have plenty of high cards, but nine tricks in no-trumps may escape you.

Love all
Dealer North

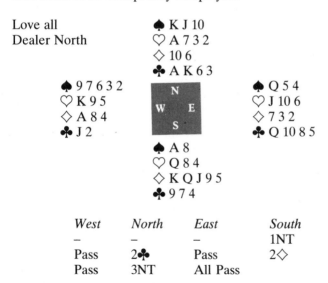

♠ K J 10
♡ A 7 3 2
◇ 10 6
♣ A K 6 3

♠ 9 7 6 3 2
♡ K 9 5
◇ A 8 4
♣ J 2

♠ Q 5 4
♡ J 10 6
◇ 7 3 2
♣ Q 10 8 5

♠ A 8
♡ Q 8 4
◇ K Q J 9 5
♣ 9 7 4

West	North	East	South
–	–	–	1NT
Pass	2♣	Pass	2◇
Pass	3NT	All Pass	

Again you prefer a weak no-trump to a suit opening. Let's imagine that West's lead of ♠ 3 is covered by the 10, queen and ace. You lead a low diamond to the 10, which holds, and return a diamond to the jack and ace. West leads a second round of spades, won in the dummy.

Now, for the first time, you are conscious of a slight *frisson*. Unless the queen of hearts provides an entry you have only seven tricks on top – three spades, one heart, one diamond and two clubs. For the moment you may as well try a heart to the queen. This loses to West's king and a third round of spades clears the suit. You are now going to make only eight tricks at best.

This unfortunate outcome could have been avoided by asking yourself the three questions we posed at the start of the chapter – how many tricks could be easily established (four, in diamonds); how could this be done (by knocking out the ace); and where might the danger lie (no subsequent entry to the South hand). Had you played the *king* of spades at trick one, the entry to the South hand would have been retained and nine tricks would have been easy.

Entries are a problem on the next deal, too. Following the theme of this chapter, the key move that declarer needs to take occurs very early in the play.

North–South game
Dealer South

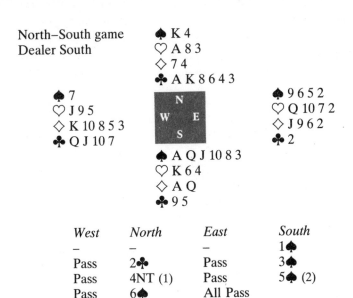

```
                    ♠ K 4
                    ♡ A 8 3
                    ◇ 7 4
                    ♣ A K 8 6 4 3
   ♠ 7                              ♠ 9 6 5 2
   ♡ J 9 5            N             ♡ Q 10 7 2
   ◇ K 10 8 5 3    W     E          ◇ J 9 6 2
   ♣ Q J 10 7         S             ♣ 2
                    ♠ A Q J 10 8 3
                    ♡ K 6 4
                    ◇ A Q
                    ♣ 9 5
```

West	North	East	South
–	–	–	1♠
Pass	2♣	Pass	3♠
Pass	4NT (1)	Pass	5♠ (2)
Pass	6♠	All Pass	

(1) Roman Key-Card Blackwood
(2) Two 'aces' and the queen of trumps

West leads the queen of clubs against your cautious small slam in spades. If clubs are 3–2 it will be easy to make all thirteen tricks. The question is . . . how can you make twelve when the cards are less favourable, with clubs 4–1 and the diamond king offside? Any ideas?

Having won the first trick with the ace of clubs you must duck a club at trick two! You can then win the return (in the South hand, if it's a heart), cross to the king of spades, and ruff a club high, establishing the suit. After you have drawn trumps the ace of hearts will provide an entry to the long clubs.

Take your time

You remember that we advised you *never* to play quickly to the first trick? Try this hand in four hearts.

Game all   ♠ A Q 5
Dealer South   ♡ J 9 5 3
                         ◇ Q 10 7 3
                         ♣ 6 4

♠ J led

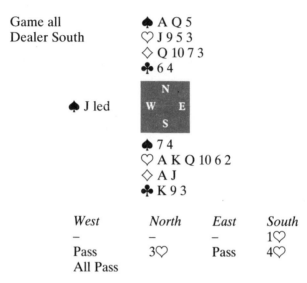

                         ♠ 7 4
                         ♡ A K Q 10 6 2
                         ◇ A J
                         ♣ K 9 3

West	North	East	South
–	–	–	1♡
Pass	3♡	Pass	4♡
All Pass			

Having noted that the clubs are a tender spot, how would you set about this contract?

Suppose you finesse the queen of spades. If this loses and East makes the obvious switch to a club, you may easily lose four tricks. But the spade finesse isn't likely to be right, is it? Players don't often lead from a king–jack–10 combination up to the strong hand. Since you would like to protect your minor-suit holdings, play *low* from dummy.

East may overtake with the king and fire through a club, but the price he pays for this will prove too high; your diamond loser will go away on the queen of spades. And suppose West's jack of spades holds the first trick. Then you follow a slightly different, but equally safe, line. You win the second spade, draw trumps, and finesse the jack of diamonds. You will lose, at most, one spade, one diamond and one club.

Q x opposite K x x at trick one

On the next deal you have to cope with a well-known type of problem that somehow is seldom easy.

North–South game
Dealer South

♠ Q 5
♡ A J 2
♢ A J 8 4 3
♣ K 7 4

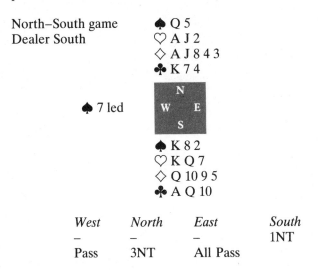

♠ 7 led

♠ K 8 2
♡ K Q 7
♢ Q 10 9 5
♣ A Q 10

West	North	East	South
–	–	–	1NT
Pass	3NT	All Pass	

Do you go up with the queen from dummy, or do you play low and let East hold the first trick with his 10 of spades? Give this some thought before you read on. With a full 31 points at your disposal and every suit well guarded, you won't want to go down in 3NT.

When the deal occurred at rubber bridge South went up with the queen of spades, which held, cashed the ace of diamonds at trick two, then played a second round of diamonds. This did not bring a smile to his partner's face, since the full hand was:

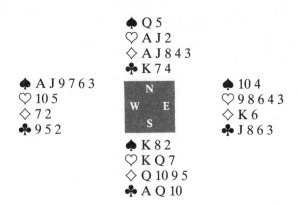

♠ Q 5
♡ A J 2
◇ A J 8 4 3
♣ K 7 4

♠ A J 9 7 6 3
♡ 10 5
◇ 7 2
♣ 9 5 2

♠ 10 4
♡ 9 8 6 4 3
◇ K 6
♣ J 8 6 3

♠ K 8 2
♡ K Q 7
◇ Q 10 9 5
♣ A Q 10

East was quick to return a spade at trick four and South was soon two down. Towards the end of the play his winners were falling on top of one another.

'That was unlucky,' South remarked. 'I played off the ace of diamonds because East might have held a singleton king; it wouldn't matter if I lost a diamond trick to West.'

What you have to look for on hands of this type is: which defender is going to win the first trick for his side? Here you can always prevent West from gaining the lead in diamonds, so East is the danger hand. You must duck the first trick. The defenders will doubtless clear the spade suit, but whenever spades are 6–2 East will have no spade to return on winning the diamond king.

If spades are 5–3 and East has the king of diamonds, there is nothing you can do. (Except to drop the king singleton, as declarer attempted; but this is only about an 8% chance, greatly inferior to finding West with six spades. After a fourth-best lead of the 7 the chance of West holding six spades must be at least 40%).

When you know where the entries lie

The winning play on the next deal would not occur to many but in fact it was clearly indicated.

Game all   ♠ K J 3
Dealer West   ♡ K 2
              ♢ J 10 4 2
              ♣ K Q 8 3

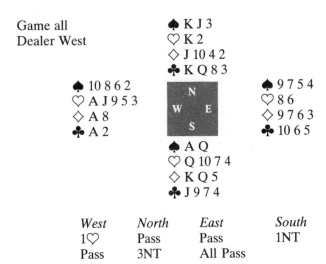

♠ 10 8 6 2   ♠ 9 7 5 4
♡ A J 9 5 3   ♡ 8 6
♢ A 8   ♢ 9 7 6 3
♣ A 2   ♣ 10 6 5

               ♠ A Q
               ♡ Q 10 7 4
               ♢ K Q 5
               ♣ J 9 7 4

West	*North*	*East*	*South*
1♡	Pass	Pass	1NT
Pass	3NT	All Pass	

West starts with ♡ 5 and you see that you will have enough tricks if you can dislodge the minor-suit aces before West can establish three tricks for himself in hearts. How will the play go?

You play low from dummy on the heart lead and win East's 8 with the 10. When you turn to one of the minors West will win with the ace and play the ace and jack of hearts. He will then be able to cash two more hearts when he takes his other ace. One down.

Since West's opening bid makes it likely that he holds all three missing aces, you can do better by rising with dummy's king of hearts at trick one. Now when West comes on lead in one of the minors he has no useful defence. Whether he leads a high or a low heart you will have three stops in the suit.

Counter-attack in trumps

Enough of no-trumps, for the moment. We'll end the chapter by looking at a few suit contracts where you must make a key move early in the play.

When you need to take ruffs in the dummy it is obvious enough that you shouldn't draw trumps prematurely. Less obvious, perhaps, is how you can prevent the defenders from doing this. The deal below was originally misplayed.

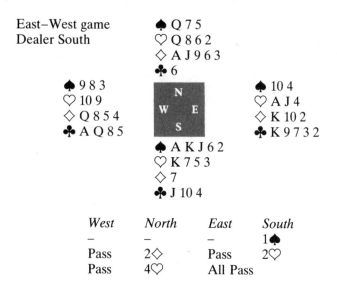

East–West game
Dealer South

♠ Q 7 5
♡ Q 8 6 2
♢ A J 9 6 3
♣ 6

♠ 9 8 3
♡ 10 9
♢ Q 8 5 4
♣ A Q 8 5

N
W E
S

♠ 10 4
♡ A J 4
♢ K 10 2
♣ K 9 7 3 2

♠ A K J 6 2
♡ K 7 5 3
♢ 7
♣ J 10 4

West	North	East	South
–	–	–	1♠
Pass	2♢	Pass	2♡
Pass	4♡	All Pass	

North's raise to game may seem a forward effort but he had three prime cards and a valuable singleton in clubs. West led the 10 of trumps and declarer had a critical play to make at trick one. Hoping that the lead was from 10 9 x, and that he might escape for one trump loser, declarer played low from dummy. East also played low and South's king won the trick.

Declarer needed two club ruffs, but when he played ♣ 10 at trick two West rose with the queen and returned another trump. East was able to pull a third round and declarer was now a trick short.

The opening lead marked East with the ace of trumps. Since declarer could afford to lose two trump tricks he should have put up dummy's queen of trumps at trick one. East must take the ace, but declarer can win the next round of trumps and is in full control. He plays on spades, aiming to throw dummy's club and ruff two clubs in the dummy. East can take his master trump when he wishes.

The theme is the same on the next hand. The defenders want to draw dummy's trumps; you are out to stop them.

East–West game
Dealer East

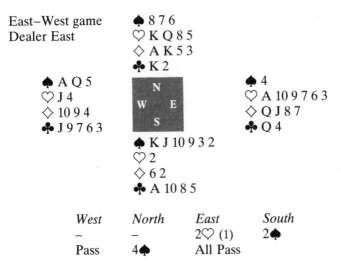

♠ 8 7 6
♡ K Q 8 5
♢ A K 5 3
♣ K 2

♠ A Q 5
♡ J 4
♢ 10 9 4
♣ J 9 7 6 3

♠ 4
♡ A 10 9 7 6 3
♢ Q J 8 7
♣ Q 4

♠ K J 10 9 3 2
♡ 2
♢ 6 2
♣ A 10 8 5

West	North	East	South
–	–	2♡ (1)	2♠
Pass	4♠	All Pass	

(1) Weak two, 6–10 points.

West leads the jack of hearts and the contract seems comfortable enough. You put on the king and East wins with the ace. What happens next is not too pleasant. East switches to a trump and West draws three rounds, depriving you of a club ruff. You've hardly had time to blink and you are one down.

If you foresee this danger you can make a clever move at trick one, playing low from dummy. If West then plays ace and another trump it will cost him a trump trick; you will still be able to ruff one club, which will give you ten tricks. It's more likely that West will switch to a diamond, but now you can take two club ruffs.

Of course, if East overtakes with the ace of hearts at trick one, to play a trump, he will pay too high a price for the privilege. You will then have two discards on dummy's heart honours. It's another example of what is known as 'avoidance play' (you remember the similar hand a while back, where ♠ J was led through A Q x and you had to duck?) You aim to prevent East, the danger hand, gaining the lead.

When trumps are short

When your trump holding is tenuous it is in the nature of defenders to put it under attack, by leading a strong side suit. It will be up to you to repel the attack.

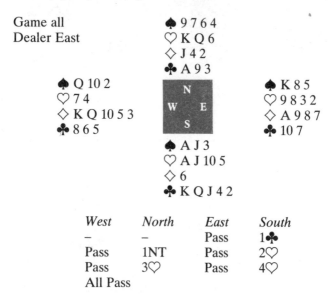

Game all
Dealer East

♠ 9 7 6 4
♡ K Q 6
♢ J 4 2
♣ A 9 3

♠ Q 10 2
♡ 7 4
♢ K Q 10 5 3
♣ 8 6 5

♠ K 8 5
♡ 9 8 3 2
♢ A 9 8 7
♣ 10 7

♠ A J 3
♡ A J 10 5
♢ 6
♣ K Q J 4 2

West	North	East	South
–	–	Pass	1♣
Pass	1NT	Pass	2♡
Pass	3♡	Pass	4♡
All Pass			

This is a type of hand which in a pairs event will be played in various contracts. Our model pair has bid competently and is installed in four hearts. West leads the king of diamonds and follows with a low diamond to the ace.

If you ruff this and play for a 3–3 trump break you will be unlucky. The sensible game is to discard spades on the second and third diamonds. Since a fourth round of diamonds can now be ruffed in the short trump hand you will be in charge unless trumps are 5–1. In that case you were never going to succeed.

If you are ready for a more difficult hand of this type, try this one:

East–West game
Dealer East

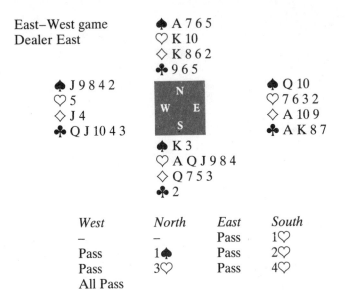

	♠ A 7 6 5		
	♡ K 10		
	◇ K 8 6 2		
	♣ 9 6 5		

♠ J 9 8 4 2   ♠ Q 10
♡ 5   ♡ 7 6 3 2
◇ J 4   ◇ A 10 9
♣ Q J 10 4 3   ♣ A K 8 7

♠ K 3
♡ A Q J 9 8 4
◇ Q 7 5 3
♣ 2

West	North	East	South
–	–	Pass	1♡
Pass	1♠	Pass	2♡
Pass	3♡	Pass	4♡
All Pass			

You may say that this is not an example of 'when trumps are short'. But when you are forced early on and the trumps break 4–1 the six-card trump suit is soon reduced to an ordinary level.

The defence to four hearts begins with two rounds of clubs and you have to ruff. Now if you start on the trump suit you will have to take four rounds, leaving you with just one trump. When the defenders win the first diamond trick they will force you again in clubs, and by this time you will have lost control.

Many quite good players would meet that fate, though the play is not difficult if you attend to the diamonds first. After a diamond to the king and ace you ruff again in clubs, then play queen and another diamond. The position is now:

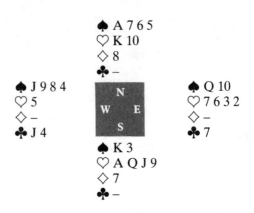

♠ A 7 6 5
♡ K 10
♢ 8
♣ –

♠ J 9 8 4
♡ 5
♢ –
♣ J 4

♠ Q 10
♡ 7 6 3 2
♢ –
♣ 7

♠ K 3
♡ A Q J 9
♢ 7
♣ –

East can do you no harm. If he leads another club you can ruff in dummy and draw trumps. And of course, if East leads a spade or a trump you make a trick with the long diamond which you have so carefully established.

2 From Here to There

Many of the more attractive plays by declarer are concerned with communications, either improving his own or playing havoc with those of the opponents. See what you make of this example. You are South playing in four spades.

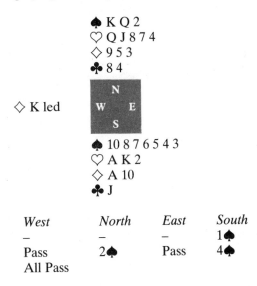

                    ♠ K Q 2
                    ♡ Q J 8 7 4
                    ♢ 9 5 3
                    ♣ 8 4

    ♢ K led

                    ♠ 10 8 7 6 5 4 3
                    ♡ A K 2
                    ♢ A 10
                    ♣ J

West	North	East	South
–	–	–	1♠
Pass	2♠	Pass	4♠
All Pass			

You win the diamond lead and play a spade to the king, on which East shows out. What now?

Perhaps you would cross to the ace of hearts to lead a second round of trumps towards dummy's queen? Not so good when the full hand turns out to be:

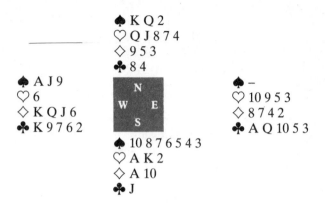

```
                    ♠ K Q 2
                    ♡ Q J 8 7 4
                    ◇ 9 5 3
                    ♣ 8 4
   ♠ A J 9                              ♠ —
   ♡ 6            N                     ♡ 10 9 5 3
   ◇ K Q J 6    W   E                   ◇ 8 7 4 2
   ♣ K 9 7 6 2    S                     ♣ A Q 10 5 3
                    ♠ 10 8 7 6 5 4 3
                    ♡ A K 2
                    ◇ A 10
                    ♣ J
```

You can see what happens. West goes up with the ace of spades and cashes the diamond queen, his partner suggesting four cards in the suit by completing a low peter. West now puts his partner in with a club (leading the 9 to show that he is not aiming to cash tricks in clubs). East returns a heart and you are one down.

It is true that the defenders might not play so accurately, but why give them the chance? When East shows out on the first spade your next play should be a *club*, destroying communication between the defending hands. It will no longer be possible for West, when he wins the ace of spades, to put his partner in for a heart ruff.

This is another hand on the same theme. Declarer ended in the second best spot but since he was doubled and the contract might have been made, this was not necessarily a bad thing.

Game all
Dealer West

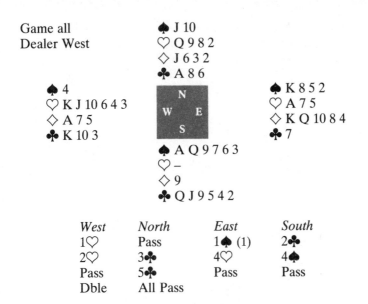

```
                    ♠ J 10
                    ♡ Q 9 8 2
                    ◇ J 6 3 2
                    ♣ A 8 6
♠ 4                                      ♠ K 8 5 2
♡ K J 10 6 4 3        N                  ♡ A 7 5
◇ A 7 5          W         E             ◇ K Q 10 8 4
♣ K 10 3              S                  ♣ 7
                    ♠ A Q 9 7 6 3
                    ♡ –
                    ◇ 9
                    ♣ Q J 9 5 4 2
```

West	North	East	South
1♡	Pass	1♠ (1)	2♣
2♡	3♣	4♡	4♠
Pass	5♣	Pass	Pass
Dble	All Pass		

(1) Not our selection, but this is how it went at the table

Four spades would have been easy, but perhaps it was difficult for North to judge this after East had responded one spade. Declarer ruffed the heart lead and led the queen of trumps, which was covered by the king and ace. The jack of spades was allowed to run and South continued with dummy's ♠ 10. East held off once more and West ruffed with the ♣ 3. Confident from the strong bidding opposite that his partner held the king of diamonds, West then underled the diamond ace. East won with the 10 and a third round of spades now promoted West's ♣ 10. That was one down.

Had declarer played a diamond at trick two there would have been no link to the East hand; the trump promotion would not have been possible. You may think that it was not too late to play a diamond after dummy's jack of spades had held. This would be true if East were to win and give his partner a spade ruff; dummy's resultant long trump would then serve to ruff a spade. But suppose East wins the diamond and exits passively with a diamond or a heart. Declarer will have no way to avoid three losers, a spade, a diamond and a trump.

You see the point of these two hands? When the defenders are threatening to establish a trump trick that doesn't really belong to them, anticipate the danger by leading the suit they will need for communication.

Discarding the danger suit

On the next deal declarer dismissed a similar communication-cutting play, thinking it would bring no benefit. The play would have gained in a different way, though.

Game all
Dealer North

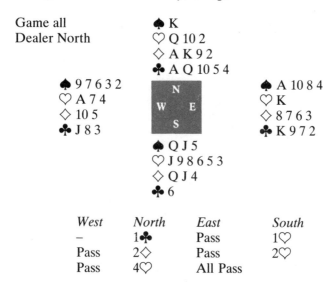

♠ K
♡ Q 10 2
◇ A K 9 2
♣ A Q 10 5 4

♠ 9 7 6 3 2
♡ A 7 4
◇ 10 5
♣ J 8 3

♠ A 10 8 4
♡ K
◇ 8 7 6 3
♣ K 9 7 2

♠ Q J 5
♡ J 9 8 6 5 3
◇ Q J 4
♣ 6

West	North	East	South
–	1♣	Pass	1♡
Pass	2◇	Pass	2♡
Pass	4♡	All Pass	

West began with ◇ 10. This looked like a doubleton (or singleton), so declarer won with the queen and hastily led a trump to East's king. East led a second round of diamonds and later came in with the ace of spades to give his partner a diamond ruff.

'It's just the same if I play on spades first,' remarked the declarer. 'They play a second diamond and East comes in with the king of hearts to give his partner the ruff.'

But that's not right! South can win the second diamond in hand, discard two diamonds on ♠ Q J, and ruff his third diamond with the queen of hearts if necessary.

A snip in time

The threat of a ruff is obvious enough on the hand below. Less easy is to see how the ruff may be avoided.

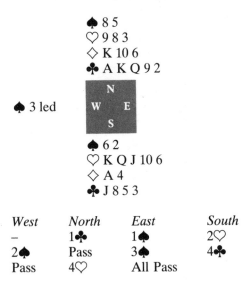

```
              ♠ 8 5
              ♡ 9 8 3
              ◇ K 10 6
              ♣ A K Q 9 2

♠ 3 led

              ♠ 6 2
              ♡ K Q J 10 6
              ◇ A 4
              ♣ J 8 5 3
```

West	North	East	South
–	1♣	1♠	2♡
2♠	Pass	3♠	4♣
Pass	4♡	All Pass	

North might well have raised the hearts at his second turn. The notion that a 'free bid' must be better than a minimum no longer has much force; no doubt he was deterred by holding three small in trumps rather than three to an honour.

Anyway, the play's the thing. East wins the spade lead with the ace and returns ♣ 7, with or without a meaning look. It is fairly clear that East has a singleton club; no doubt he hopes to come in with the ace of hearts, put his partner in with a spade, and ruff the second round of clubs. Can you do anything about this?

Well, you can try. It is possible that East holds both the queen and jack of diamonds. So what about cashing the top two diamonds, then playing ◇ 10, throwing your second spade? This will work well, since the full hand is:

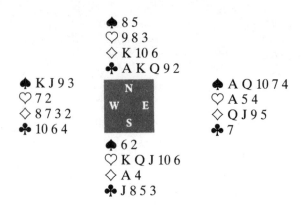

You will lose just one spade, one heart and one diamond. The play is known as a 'Scissors Coup', because declarer cuts the lifeline between the two defenders.

Clearing the blockage

It's time to look at declarer's own communications. This deal from a Gold Cup semi-final is a classic example of how small and inconspicuous cards can play an important role.

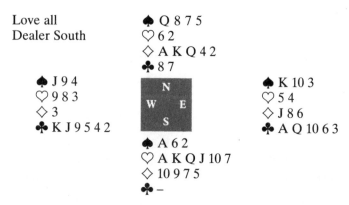

At one table North–South played in six diamonds and needed just one club ruff to land an overtrick. At the other table South arrived in six hearts and a club was led. Who is going to gain on the board? The man in hearts because 980 beats 940?

The declarer in six hearts ruffed the club lead and drew trumps in three rounds, discarding the second club from dummy. Then disaster struck. The diamonds were blocked and after four rounds of the suit South had to play for a little luck in spades, which was not forthcoming.

'When West showed out on the second diamond, couldn't you have ducked in dummy?' demanded North. 'Then you can run the rest of the diamonds.'

'So I can,' replied South. 'But I can discard only one spade and I'm still a trick short.'

North felt there must have been some way to make the slam, and so there was. The mistake lay in discarding ♣ 8 from dummy on the third round of hearts! So long as declarer keeps that card he can draw trumps, play just two rounds of diamonds, then lead ♣ 8 and discard the obstreperous fourth diamond from the South hand.

In case this play struck you earlier, you might also have succeeded by discarding a diamond on the club lead at trick one!

Delaying the entry

The winning line on the last deal would have been neat play. Another hand from the same match also proved tricky.

Game all   ♠ 10 7
Dealer East   ♡ 9 6 4
               ◇ K 4
               ♣ A J 9 6 3 2

♠ 9 8 2   ♠ A K Q 5 4
♡ 8 3   ♡ Q 7
◇ J 9 8 6   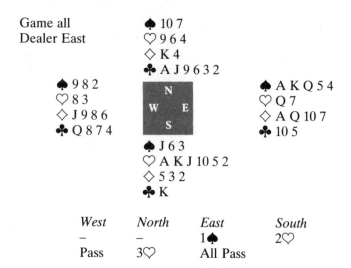   ◇ A Q 10 7
♣ Q 8 7 4   ♣ 10 5

               ♠ J 6 3
               ♡ A K J 10 5 2
               ◇ 5 3 2
               ♣ K

West	North	East	South
–	–	1♠	2♡
Pass	3♡	All Pass	

North's three-heart call was well judged. If instead he bids three
clubs, as many players would, he won't know what to do over
South's likely rebid of three hearts.

West led ♠ 9 and East played three rounds, forcing dummy to
ruff. South picked up the trumps successfully and tried hard for
an end-play of some kind, but he had to lose three tricks at the
finish.

'. . . forcing dummy to ruff.' Did you notice that? Instead,
South should discard a diamond from dummy on the third spade.
If East now cashes the ace of diamonds and plays a fourth round
of spades you will ruff with the jack, unblock the club king, and
ruff a diamond to reach the ace of clubs. If instead East switches
to a trump, you win with the ace, cash the king of clubs and
concede a diamond, again reaching dummy with a diamond ruff.

Keeping the dummy alive

When the pathway to dummy is precarious declarer must sometimes take special steps to keep it in good repair.

East–West game
Dealer South

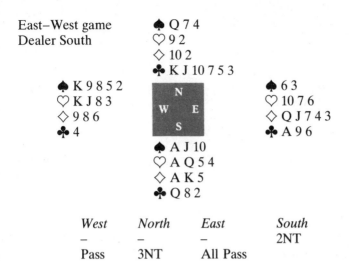

♠ Q 7 4
♡ 9 2
◇ 10 2
♣ K J 10 7 5 3

♠ K 9 8 5 2
♡ K J 8 3
◇ 9 8 6
♣ 4

♠ 6 3
♡ 10 7 6
◇ Q J 7 4 3
♣ A 9 6

♠ A J 10
♡ A Q 5 4
◇ A K 5
♣ Q 8 2

West	North	East	South
–	–	–	2NT
Pass	3NT	All Pass	

West leads ♠ 5 and declarer wins with the 10. What now? The answer is that he will go at least one down. East will hold up the ace of clubs for two rounds and dummy's club suit will be dead.

A better idea is to win with the *ace* of spades at trick one. Now East's hold-up in clubs will be ineffective. The queen of spades will provide an entry to dummy's remaining clubs, giving declarer ten tricks. Plays of this type are usually easy to execute, once the idea has occurred to you.

The same manoeuvre, winning with an unnecessarily high card, can occur in a trump contract.

Game all   ♠ 10 9 8 3
Dealer South   ♡ 5
              ◇ A J 9 7 6 3 2
              ♣ 8

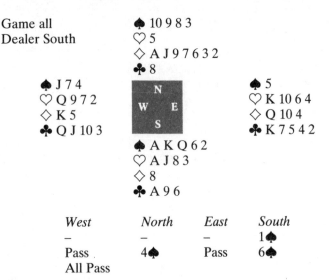

♠ J 7 4   ♠ 5
♡ Q 9 7 2   ♡ K 10 6 4
◇ K 5   ◇ Q 10 4
♣ Q J 10 3   ♣ K 7 5 4 2

              ♠ A K Q 6 2
              ♡ A J 8 3
              ◇ 8
              ♣ A 9 6

West	*North*	*East*	*South*
–	–	–	1♠
Pass	4♠	Pass	6♠
All Pass			

West leads the queen of clubs and your first thought may be of a cross-ruff. You would need to score all nine trumps separately, though, and would probably run into an overruff at some stage.

How about setting up the diamonds? Since there are not many entries to dummy the idea may come to mind of ruffing the second round of diamonds with a *high* trump; by retaining two low trumps you would then be sure of an extra entry to dummy in the trump suit.

So, cross to the ace of diamonds and ruff a diamond with the ace. Cash the king of trumps and continue with a low trump. West may win with the jack and force the dummy with a second round of clubs. You can now ruff a diamond with the queen and cross to dummy's ♠ 10, drawing West's last trump. The table is high.

Finessing to gain entry

Sometimes a suit that contains no losers can be played in a special way to create extra entries. Look at these two holdings:

(1) A J 4 3   (2) A 9 3

K Q 10 2   K Q J 6 5

Suppose in both cases you need entries to the North hand. On (1) you cash the king, then overtake the queen with the ace. If both defenders follow, you will be able to overtake the 10 with the jack on the next round, setting up the 4 as a third entry in the suit. On (2) you have the option of finessing dummy's 9 if you need a second entry.

Here is a somewhat exotic example of gaining an entry by taking an 'unnecessary' finesse.

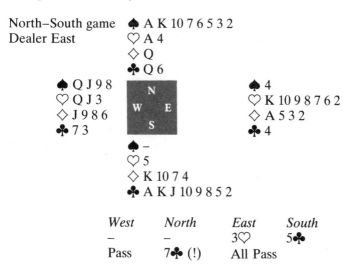

North–South game ♠ A K 10 7 6 5 3 2
Dealer East   ♡ A 4
                 ♢ Q
                 ♣ Q 6

♠ Q J 9 8   ♠ 4
♡ Q J 3   ♡ K 10 9 8 7 6 2
♢ J 9 8 6   ♢ A 5 3 2
♣ 7 3   ♣ 4

                ♠ –
                ♡ 5
                ♢ K 10 7 4
                ♣ A K J 10 9 8 5 2

West	North	East	South
–	–	3♡	5♣
Pass	7♣ (!)	All Pass	

It may have the air of a constructed hand but it was actually dealt at the table. Had North wished to bid the hand scientifically, five hearts would have been his call. He blasted straight to the grand, though, and West led the queen of hearts, won in the dummy.

Declarer now had to set up the spade suit. He needed trumps to be 2–1, regardless, but the exact line of play depended on how the spades broke.

Declarer cashed the ace of spades at trick 2, then led another spade. When East showed out, he ruffed high in the South hand and led the 2 of trumps. The 3 came from West and declarer finessed the 6. When East followed resignedly with the 4, all was well. Declarer could now ruff another spade high and cross to the queen of clubs to enjoy the spades. If spades had been 3–2, of course, the finesse in trumps would not have been needed.

Do you see why declarer had to ruff the second round of spades high? Had he ruffed with the 2 and then proffered the 5, West could have killed the second trump entry by going in with the 7!

Even the mighty

Every beginner is taught that with such as A x opposite K Q J x you should cash the honour in the short holding first, to aid your communications. This lesson should perhaps be heeded in higher places too. Look at the next hand.

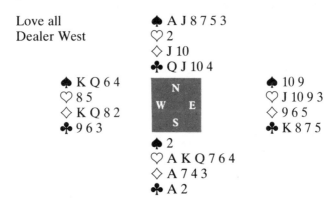

Love all
Dealer West

♠ A J 8 7 5 3
♡ 2
♢ J 10
♣ Q J 10 4

♠ K Q 6 4
♡ 8 5
♢ K Q 8 2
♣ 9 6 3

♠ 10 9
♡ J 10 9 3
♢ 9 6 5
♣ K 8 7 5

♠ 2
♡ A K Q 7 6 4
♢ A 7 4 3
♣ A 2

You play in four hearts and West leads ♣ 6. You must play the 4 from dummy and win with the *ace*. After three rounds of trumps, revealing the 4–2 break, the way is clear for a small club to the queen. When you regain the lead you can cross to the ace of spades and throw two losers on dummy's clubs, not minding if East can ruff the fourth round.

'Easy enough,' you may say. 'No good player would block the suit by playing a high club from dummy at trick 1.'

You don't think so? Not even the Italian maestro, D'Alelio, playing in the 1969 Bermuda Bowl against the USA?

3 *Make* Them *Play*

Has it ever struck you that it is never an advantage to make the first play in a suit? If a trick will go well for you when you lead, it will go at least as well if one of the opponents has to make the first play. Take a simple situation like this:

♠ Q J 9

♠ 10 6 4   ♠ K 8 7 3

♠ A 5 2

If either opponent has to broach this suit South will make all three tricks. If declarer has to open the suit East will refuse to cover the first honour played from dummy; declarer will be held to two tricks, unless he can arrange a subsequent end-play of some sort.

The very common manoeuvre known as 'elimination play' exploits this situation. The opponents are put in a position where they have to lead a suit to their disadvantage. There are many familiar combinations where declarer would much prefer the opposition to make the first play:

(1) ♣ Q 5 2   (2) ◇ K 6 4   (3) ♡ A 7 3

♣ J 7 3   ◇ J 7 2   ♡ J 10 4

In all these cases your prospects of tricks will mushroom if the opponents have to make the first lead. How can you persuade them to do this? By throwing them in at a time when they have no safe alternative. That's the subject of the present chapter.

Eliminate and exit

We'll look first at a relatively straightforward hand where declarer eliminates two side suits and exits in the third, where two losers were possible.

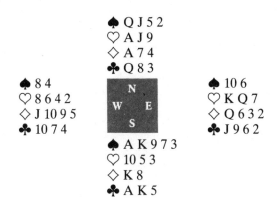

♠ Q J 5 2
♡ A J 9
◇ A 7 4
♣ Q 8 3

♠ 8 4
♡ 8 6 4 2
◇ J 10 9 5
♣ 10 7 4

♠ 10 6
♡ K Q 7
◇ Q 6 3 2
♣ J 9 6 2

♠ A K 9 7 3
♡ 10 5 3
◇ K 8
♣ A K 5

South plays in six spades and West makes the natural lead of ◇ J. South wins with the king and draws trumps in two rounds. An inexperienced player might proceed to take two heart finesses, not thinking much of his luck when both the king and queen turned up offside.

It's a simple matter to make a certainty of the contract. After drawing trumps, you ruff the third round of diamonds (eliminating the suit) and cash three clubs (eliminating that suit). You will have arrived at this position:

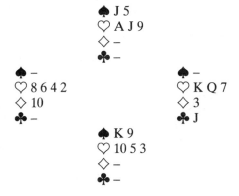

♠ J 5
♡ A J 9
◇ –
♣ –

♠ –
♡ 8 6 4 2
◇ 10
♣ –

♠ –
♡ K Q 7
◇ 3
♣ J

♠ K 9
♡ 10 5 3
◇ –
♣ –

Now a low heart is led to the jack. When East wins he is 'on play', forced to return a heart into the tenace or to concede a ruff-and-discard. The play would be described as a 'ruff-and-discard elimination'.

Quite right, partner!

This is a slightly more tricky deal of the same type:

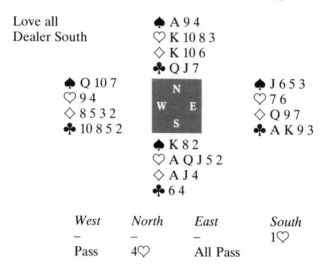

Love all
Dealer South

♠ A 9 4
♡ K 10 8 3
♢ K 10 6
♣ Q J 7

♠ Q 10 7
♡ 9 4
♢ 8 5 3 2
♣ 10 8 5 2

♠ J 6 5 3
♡ 7 6
♢ Q 9 7
♣ A K 9 3

♠ K 8 2
♡ A Q J 5 2
♢ A J 4
♣ 6 4

West	North	East	South
–	–	–	1♡
Pass	4♡	All Pass	

A response of 3NT would have worked well on the North cards, but that sort of call sometimes turns out badly (not to mention the fact that partner may claim you're trying to hog the bidding).

When the deal first occurred, West began with a spade to the jack and king. Declarer drew trumps in two rounds, then played a club to the queen and king. East dislodged the second spade stopper and declarer returned to the South hand for another club lead. When the jack lost to the king the defenders took their spade trick and exited safely with a third round of clubs. You won't be surprised to hear that declarer then misguessed the diamonds, going one down.

'What a nightmare,' complained South. 'Everything was wrong.'

'Quite so,' remarked his partner. 'Including the way you played it.'

The simple game, after drawing trumps, is to continue spades, playing ace and another. Now the contract cannot fail.

Suppose that West wins and leads a club. The jack will lose to the king and East will be on play, forced to concede a ruff-and-discard or give a trick in one or other minor.

When to exit

With a 5–5 trump fit on the next hand it's natural to think of elimination play once again. What should the order of play be, though? The contract is four spades and West leads a trump.

Love all
Dealer South

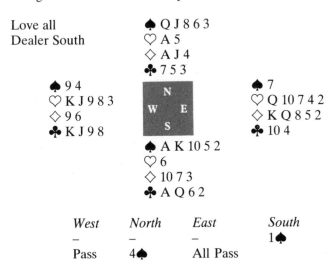

```
                ♠ Q J 8 6 3
                ♡ A 5
                ◇ A J 4
                ♣ 7 5 3
♠ 9 4                              ♠ 7
♡ K J 9 8 3                        ♡ Q 10 7 4 2
◇ 9 6                              ◇ K Q 8 5 2
♣ K J 9 8                         ♣ 10 4
                ♠ A K 10 5 2
                ♡ 6
                ◇ 10 7 3
                ♣ A Q 6 2
```

West	North	East	South
–	–	–	1♠
Pass	4♠	All Pass	

If you haven't met the type before you may not find it easy. There's only one line that guarantees the contract. You must win the trump lead, draw the remaining trump, then eliminate the hearts. No problem so far. The next move is to play ace and another club. However the clubs lie, the winner of this trick will not be able to play on clubs without giving you a second trick in the suit. Nor can the defenders safely play diamonds. Suppose that West is in and leads a diamond to his partner's queen. East will be end-played, forced to return a diamond into dummy's tenace or to concede a ruff-and-discard.

Slight slip

The declarer had a good plan on the next deal, but he was guilty of a small oversight.

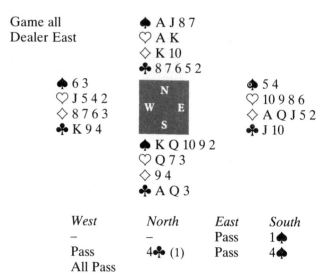

Game all
Dealer East

♠ A J 8 7
♡ A K
♢ K 10
♣ 8 7 6 5 2

♠ 6 3
♡ J 5 4 2
♢ 8 7 6 3
♣ K 9 4

♠ 5 4
♡ 10 9 8 6
♢ A Q J 5 2
♣ J 10

♠ K Q 10 9 2
♡ Q 7 3
♢ 9 4
♣ A Q 3

West	North	East	South
–	–	Pass	1♠
Pass	4♣ (1)	Pass	4♠
All Pass			

(1) A variant of Swiss, sound raise to game with two aces.

West led a diamond against four spades and East cashed two diamonds, then tried the jack of clubs. Since there was no need to finesse at this point, and in any case the lack of an opening bid from East suggested ♣ K was offside, declarer went up with the ace. At this point he had a plan: he cashed ♡ A K, drew trumps in two rounds, then played ♡ Q, discarding a club from dummy. The position was now:

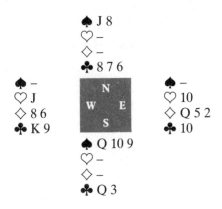

♠ J 8
♡ –
◇ –
♣ 8 7 6

♠ –
♡ J
◇ 8 6
♣ K 9

♠ –
♡ 10
◇ Q 5 2
♣ 10

♠ Q 10 9
♡ –
◇ –
♣ Q 3

Declarer crossed to dummy with a trump and led a club from the table. You can see his idea: even if the king were offside the opponents would be end-played if East had the bare ♣ 10 at this stage, or West the bare ♣ K. Unfortunately, something went wrong. When declarer crossed to dummy with a trump, East discarded his 10 of clubs! West's ♣ K 9 were then sitting comfortably over declarer's queen.

Do you see declarer's mistake? It was the third round of trumps that caused his downfall; he should have crossed to dummy by ruffing the queen of hearts instead. East would then have had no chance to dispose of his ♣ 10.

Wrong from the start

Declarer went wrong on this deal too, not that it was a particularly easy hand to play.

North–South game
Dealer West

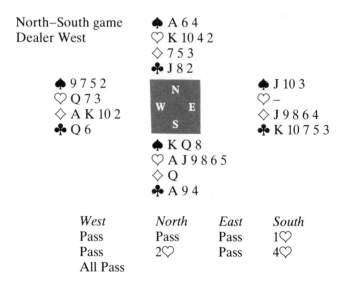

♠ A 6 4
♡ K 10 4 2
♢ 7 5 3
♣ J 8 2

♠ 9 7 5 2
♡ Q 7 3
♢ A K 10 2
♣ Q 6

♠ J 10 3
♡ –
♢ J 9 8 6 4
♣ K 10 7 5 3

♠ K Q 8
♡ A J 9 8 6 5
♢ Q
♣ A 9 4

West	North	East	South
Pass	Pass	Pass	1♡
Pass	2♡	Pass	4♡
All Pass			

West started with his top diamonds. South ruffed the second round and led a low heart to the king. Wrong view! Declarer decided at this point that his best chance might be to find West with a doubleton Q x or K x of clubs and to end-play him at the finish. He ruffed dummy's last diamond, then cashed the ace of hearts and three rounds of spades. This led to:

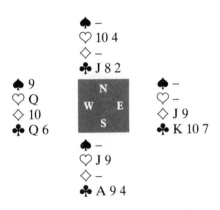

```
            ♠ —
            ♡ 10 4
            ◇ —
            ♣ J 8 2
♠ 9                        ♠ —
♡ Q          N            ♡ —
◇ 10      W     E         ◇ J 9
♣ Q 6         S           ♣ K 10 7
            ♠ —
            ♡ J 9
            ◇ —
            ♣ A 9 4
```

South now attempted his end-play by leading ace and another club. West, although not a very experienced player, had the wit to throw the queen under the ace and so escaped the throw-in. South lost a heart, a diamond and two clubs.

Does South deserve our sympathy, do you think, or might he have played better? First, let's look at his opening gambit in the trump suit – low to the king. Which defender, if either, was likely to be void in trumps? West had passed originally, had not intervened over the one heart opening, and had turned up with a suit of diamonds headed by the ace–king. Had he been void of hearts he might well have intervened on the second round, with a double or a bid of two diamonds. The ace of hearts first, playing East for the possible void, would therefore have made better sense.

Secondly, there was no need to give West the chance to unblock in clubs. After his mis-guess in trumps South should have ruffed the third diamond and led a low club from hand. Suppose that West goes up with the queen and leads another. It would be quite easy now to cash the ace of hearts, play off three spades, then exit with a heart to the queen. West would have to concede a ruff-and-discard.

Partial Elimination

In most of the examples so far, it has been possible to remove completely the suits that would give the defender a safe exit. Sometimes this is not possible and you have to hope that the player who is thrown in will be unable to exit safely.

The technique is known as a partial elimination. This example comes from the 1993 European Championship, with the Netherlands facing Poland.

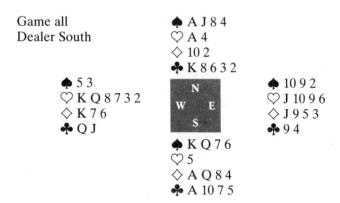

Game all
Dealer South

North:
♠ A J 8 4
♡ A 4
◇ 10 2
♣ K 8 6 3 2

West:
♠ 5 3
♡ K Q 8 7 3 2
◇ K 7 6
♣ Q J

East:
♠ 10 9 2
♡ J 10 9 6
◇ J 9 5 3
♣ 9 4

South:
♠ K Q 7 6
♡ 5
◇ A Q 8 4
♣ A 10 7 5

South, Muller for the Netherlands, ended in six spades after West had overcalled in hearts. He won the king of hearts lead with the ace, drew just two rounds of trumps, and ruffed dummy's remaining heart. He then crossed to the king of clubs, the queen falling from West.

The percentage play on the second round of clubs is to finesse the 10. (This is because if West started with Q J he might have chosen to play the jack instead of the queen; with a singleton queen he would have no choice in the matter.) Muller duly proceeded to take the club finesse. This lost to the jack, but thanks to declarer's earlier preparations West now had no safe exit. He returned a diamond and twelve tricks resulted.

Note that declarer's line was secure also if the club queen had been singleton. If West had ruffed ♣ 10 with the outstanding trump he would then have been end-played.

You might think such a hand not too difficult for an international player, but strangely the Polish declarer went two down in the same contract! Mind you, this didn't stop Poland winning the championship.

Loser-on-loser throw-in

One of the most elegant plays in the game is the so-called loser-on-loser throw-in. This is a fairly straightforward example:

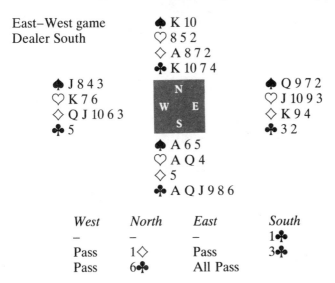

East–West game
Dealer South

♠ K 10
♡ 8 5 2
♢ A 8 7 2
♣ K 10 7 4

♠ J 8 4 3
♡ K 7 6
♢ Q J 10 6 3
♣ 5

♠ Q 9 7 2
♡ J 10 9 3
♢ K 9 4
♣ 3 2

♠ A 6 5
♡ A Q 4
♢ 5
♣ A Q J 9 8 6

West	North	East	South
–	–	–	1♣
Pass	1♢	Pass	3♣
Pass	6♣	All Pass	

Your partner obviously belongs to the old-fashioned 'bid what you think you can make' school. Nothing wrong with that, when it works. Anyway, West leads the queen of diamonds against six clubs and you win with the ace in dummy. Whether or not you have a vision of how the play may develop, it is natural to ruff a diamond at trick two, draw the trumps in two rounds, and ruff another diamond.

On the third round of diamonds East plays the king; West, who threw one diamond on the second round of trumps, contributes a mildly deceptive jack. There is not much doubt where the last diamond is, though. You cash the king and ace of spades, then ruff a spade to reach this position:

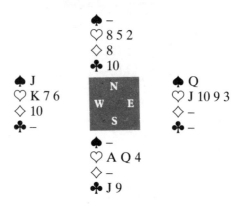

Now, of course, you don't finesse in hearts. You lead the fourth diamond from dummy and discard a losing heart. End of story.

While we are on the subject, loser-on-loser play may be used in a different cause – to keep a dangerous defender out of the lead while you set up a suit.

Game all
Dealer South

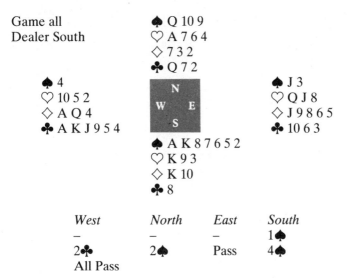

♠ Q 10 9
♡ A 7 6 4
♢ 7 3 2
♣ Q 7 2

♠ 4
♡ 10 5 2
♢ A Q 4
♣ A K J 9 5 4

♠ J 3
♡ Q J 8
♢ J 9 8 6 5
♣ 10 6 3

♠ A K 8 7 6 5 2
♡ K 9 3
♢ K 10
♣ 8

West	North	East	South
–	–	–	1♠
2♣	2♠	Pass	4♠
All Pass			

West led the ace of clubs and switched to his singleton trump, covered by the 9, jack and king. Declarer saw that if he drew the outstanding trump and simply gave up a heart, East might win the heart trick and fire through a diamond. On the actual layout this would have led to one down, even though hearts were 3–3.

South could see a better idea. He crossed to dummy with a second trump and led the queen of clubs, discarding a heart. West, the safe hand, won the club trick and declarer was later able to ruff the thirteenth heart good and reach it with a trump.

A well-played hand, would you say? There was actually a much better line available, one that would win also if West had only two hearts. The first move is to cross to a trump and ruff a club. The king and ace of hearts follow and only then does declarer lead the queen of clubs, throwing his last heart. If hearts are 3–3 West will have to play a heart, allowing the thirteenth card to be ruffed good, or concede a trick in one of the minors. If West started with fewer than three hearts he will have to exit in a minor anyway.

Safe on one side

The prospect of elimination play later in the hand will sometimes dictate how the trump suit should be played.

Love all
Dealer South

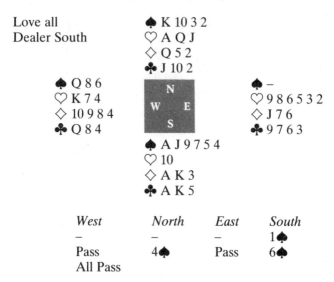

♠ K 10 3 2
♡ A Q J
◇ Q 5 2
♣ J 10 2

♠ Q 8 6
♡ K 7 4
◇ 10 9 8 4
♣ Q 8 4

♠ –
♡ 9 8 6 5 3 2
◇ J 7 6
♣ 9 7 6 3

♠ A J 9 7 5 4
♡ 10
◇ A K 3
♣ A K 5

West	North	East	South
–	–	–	1♠
Pass	4♠	Pass	6♠
All Pass			

West led a diamond and declarer won with the ace, noting that the two black queens were his only problem. There was no clue to which defender might be short in spades, but declarer could see that a trump to the king would guarantee the contract; if East were to show out it would be possible later to end-play West.

When East did show out on the first round of trumps declarer drew a second round. He then cashed the remaining two diamonds, followed by the ace of hearts. West was put on lead with the trump queen and found himself with no safe return.

Had declarer opened the trump suit by cashing the ace the contract would not have been secure. When East was thrown in with a trump he would exit in clubs, forcing declarer to guess which finesse to take – hearts or clubs.

Safe on both sides

The 'elimination play' aquarium contains a few exotic specimens. On the next deal a special lie of the heart suit made it possible to play loser-on-loser against either opponent. Some detective work in another suit was required before deciding which throw-in would be needed.

East–West game
Dealer North

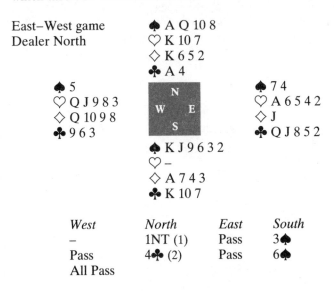

♠ A Q 10 8
♡ K 10 7
◇ K 6 5 2
♣ A 4

♠ 5
♡ Q J 9 8 3
◇ Q 10 9 8
♣ 9 6 3

♠ 7 4
♡ A 6 5 4 2
◇ J
♣ Q J 8 5 2

♠ K J 9 6 3 2
♡ –
◇ A 7 4 3
♣ K 10 7

West	North	East	South
–	1NT (1)	Pass	3♠
Pass	4♣ (2)	Pass	6♠
All Pass			

(1) 16–18 points
(2) Cue bid, with good spade support

West started with the queen of hearts and declarer played low from dummy, ruffing in the South hand. After drawing trumps he played off the ace and king of diamonds. Had the suit broken 3–2 he would simply have conceded a diamond. As it was, he had to turn his mind to end-playing East, the defender with no diamonds left.

Declarer ruffed ♡ 10, eliminated clubs, then led ♡ K. When East covered, a diamond was thrown from the South hand. East had to give a ruff-and-discard and away went declarer's last diamond.

The play would be similar if East were the man with four diamonds. On the second round of hearts declarer would lead the king, covered and ruffed. He would then be able to end-play West with ♡ 10.

Never too early

It pays to keep awake at this game. Italian maestro Pietro Forquet made four hearts on the following deal by end-playing West. The opening lead was the king of spades.

Game all
Dealer West

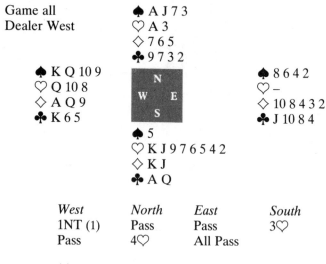

```
                  ♠ A J 7 3
                  ♡ A 3
                  ♢ 7 6 5
                  ♣ 9 7 3 2
♠ K Q 10 9                        ♠ 8 6 4 2
♡ Q 10 8            N             ♡ –
♢ A Q 9       W         E         ♢ 10 8 4 3 2
♣ K 6 5            S              ♣ J 10 8 4
                  ♠ 5
                  ♡ K J 9 7 6 5 4 2
                  ♢ K J
                  ♣ A Q
```

West	North	East	South
1NT (1)	Pass	Pass	3♡
Pass	4♡	All Pass	

(1) 16–18 points

The bidding allowed Forquet to place every outstanding honour with West. He saw that he could underwrite the contract simply by allowing the spade king to win! Since all four suits represented an unsafe exit for the poor defender in the West seat, no further elimination was needed.

4 Special Moves in Trump Contracts

The presence of a trump suit always adds an extra dimension to the play of the cards and in this chapter we cast an eye over some of the special manoeuvres which become possible.

About turn

Suppose that you have a trump holding of this type:

♠ A Q 9

♠ K J 10 4 3

You start with five tricks and if you can manage one or two ruffs with the short trump holding you will be able to boost this to six or seven trump tricks.

What will the effect be of taking ruffs in the long holding, though? If you take only one or two ruffs you will score just the five tricks that you had at the start. To gain a trick by ruffing in the long hand you would need to take *three* ruffs there. Three trump tricks (in the dummy), plus three ruffs in your hand, would bring the total to six. That's the idea behind the technique known as 'dummy reversal'.

Let's look at a complete deal featuring the trump holding above:

North–South game
Dealer North

```
                    ♠ A Q 9
                    ♡ A K 8 2
                    ◇ 10 6 4
                    ♣ A 9 5
  ♠ 8 7 2                        ♠ 6 5
  ♡ J 6              N           ♡ Q 10 9 7 4
  ◇ K J 9 2      W     E         ◇ Q 8
  ♣ Q 10 4 3         S           ♣ K J 7 2
                    ♠ K J 10 4 3
                    ♡ 5 3
                    ◇ A 7 5 3
                    ♣ 8 6
```

West	North	East	South
–	1♡	Pass	1♠
Pass	2NT	Pass	3◇
Pass	3♠	Pass	4♠
All Pass			

3NT would have been easy but South decided to try his luck in four spades. There are four winners outside the trump suit and if South can achieve one ruff in the dummy he will score six trump tricks, bringing his total to ten. West makes the bright start of a trump, though, after which he will be able to stop South ruffing the fourth round of diamonds.

What now? Declarer sees that if he can ruff two hearts and a club in his own hand he will again score the six trump tricks that he needs. He wins the trump lead in dummy, cashes the two top hearts and ruffs a heart high. After cashing the ace of diamonds he plays a club to the ace and ruffs dummy's last heart, again with a high trump. He surrenders a club now and the defenders play a second round of trumps. This is won in the dummy and declarer ruffs a club in the South hand. He has scored nine tricks and the top trump on the table will be the tenth.

Not many players would think of dummy reversal on the next deal, where the trump holding is 6–3.

Game all
Dealer North

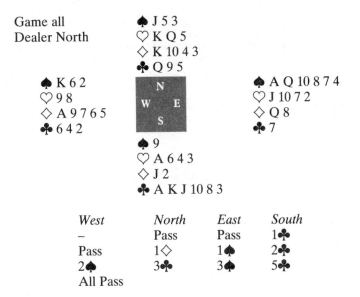

	♠ J 5 3		
	♡ K Q 5		
	◇ K 10 4 3		
	♣ Q 9 5		
♠ K 6 2			♠ A Q 10 8 7 4
♡ 9 8			♡ J 10 7 2
◇ A 9 7 6 5			◇ Q 8
♣ 6 4 2			♣ 7
	♠ 9		
	♡ A 6 4 3		
	◇ J 2		
	♣ A K J 10 8 3		

West	North	East	South
–	Pass	Pass	1♣
Pass	1◇	1♠	2♣
2♠	3♣	3♠	5♣
All Pass			

West leads a spade to the ace and South ruffs the spade return.
What's the best play at trick three, do you think? The two of
diamonds, surely, because this will put West under pressure if he
holds the ace. West plays well, however. Since declarer had only
one spade he surely has at least two diamonds; so West plays low.
South, reflecting that East passed originally, nevertheless takes
the right view, playing the king from dummy.

Dummy's last spade is ruffed high and the jack of diamonds is
played to East's queen. When East returns a trump South wins
with the ace and crosses to dummy by overtaking ♣ 8 with the 9.
A diamond ruff is followed by a heart to the king and another
diamond ruff with South's last trump. A heart to the queen
allows the last trump to be drawn and the dummy reversal is
complete.

Even though South started with six trumps in his hand and only
three in the dummy, it was possible to gain a trick by ruffing in the
long trump hand. That's because he took *four* ruffs there, giving
him a total of seven trump tricks.

It is a deal with several instructive points: the early diamond
lead, West's decision to play low, the play of the king from
dummy; then the two diamond ruffs, leading to a dummy reversal.

Playing a cross-ruff

Another way to make the most of your trump suit is to score the trumps separately, the familiar cross-ruff. Consider this play whenever you have a marked shortage in both hands.

North–South game
Dealer South

		♠ 7		
		♡ A Q 6 4		
		◇ A 10 5 3 2		
		♣ 8 7 3		
♠ K Q J 9 2		**N**		♠ 8 6 4
♡ 2	**W**		**E**	♡ 10 9 8 5
◇ Q 9 4		**S**		◇ K J 7 6
♣ J 10 5 4				♣ Q 2
		♠ A 10 5 3		
		♡ K J 7 3		
		◇ 8		
		♣ A K 9 6		

West	North	East	South
–	–	–	1♣
1♠	Dble (1)	Pass	3♡
Pass	4NT (2)	Pass	5♣ (3)
Pass	6♡	All Pass	

(1) In the tournament world these low-level doubles are 'negative', not for penalties
(2) Roman Key-card Blackwood
(3) 0 or 3 of the five 'aces' (including the king of the likely trump suit)

North takes a forward view of his hand and puts his partner into six hearts. A trump lead would be best but West looks no further than the spade king, won in the South hand.

Declarer now considers the possibility of a cross-ruff. He has four winners outside the trump suit, so will need to score all eight trumps to bring his total to twelve. In fact, this simplifies the plan; he will have to attempt four low ruffs followed by four high ruffs.

Declarer crosses to the ace of diamonds, ruffs a diamond low, ruffs a spade low, then ruffs a second diamond low. Although, after West's overcall, there is a risk of an overruff, declarer must now ruff another spade low. When these ruffs pass by without misadventure he is home.

Well, almost home, we should say. What would happen if he continued with a diamond ruffed high, followed by a spade ruffed high? East would discard a club! It would then be too late for declarer to score his two club winners. To avoid such a disaster the declarer in a cross-ruff should always cash his side-suit winners at the earliest convenient moment. On the present hand South should cash the ace and king of clubs immediately after winning the opening lead.

So, these are the three points to remember about playing a cross-ruff:

(i) Count your tricks, to see how many ruffing tricks you will need.

(ii) Calculate how many ruffs with low trumps are required, and in which hand they should be taken.

(iii) Unless they are needed for entry, cash your winners in the side suits before embarking on the cross-ruff.

With these ideas fresh in the mind, let's tackle another cross-ruff hand.

North–South game

Dealer South

	♠ A K 8 7 2	
	♡ Q J 8 5	
	◇ 4	
	♣ A 7 3	

♠ J 3		♠ Q 10 9 6 4
♡ 6 4	N	♡ 10 9 3
◇ Q 10 6 5 3	W E	◇ J 8
♣ J 10 5 2	S	♣ Q 8 6

	♠ 5	
	♡ A K 7 2	
	◇ A K 9 7 2	
	♣ K 9 4	

West	*North*	*East*	*South*
–	–	–	1◇
Pass	1♠	Pass	2♡
Pass	4♣	Pass	4NT
Pass	5♠	Pass	5NT
Pass	6◇	Pass	6♡
All Pass			

South launches into Roman Key-Card Blackwood when the
heart fit comes to light. His 5NT continuation tells partner that
all the top cards are present but North, with an unhelpful holding
in diamonds, declines to bid the grand.

West leads a trump, which runs to the 10 and king, and
declarer now considers the prospects of a cross-ruff. He has six
side-suit winners and one trump trick already made, so he needs
only *five* more trump tricks.

If declarer can manage one low ruff, with the 2, he can take the
next three ruffs with master trumps; he will then be left with the 7
and 8 of trumps, equals against the 9 and certain to produce a
twelfth trick.

The first move is to cash the three ace–king combinations in
the side suits, discarding a club from the South hand and a spade
from the North hand. Declarer must now judge which is the safer
ruff to take with the 2, a club or a spade. The fall, offside, of the
jack of spades should lead him to play for a low ruff in clubs (one
club was thrown on the spades, remember). When this succeeds,
twelve tricks are assured.

Trumps under attack

When a defender holds four trumps, or suspects that his partner does, he will usually attack in a suit that the defenders hold strongly. Back in Chapter 1 we saw some of the basic counter-measures available to declarer. On the next couple of deals it is somewhat more difficult to keep the defenders at bay.

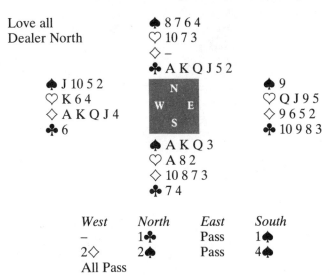

Love all
Dealer North

♠ 8 7 6 4
♡ 10 7 3
♢ –
♣ A K Q J 5 2

♠ J 10 5 2
♡ K 6 4
♢ A K Q J 4
♣ 6

♠ 9
♡ Q J 9 5
♢ 9 6 5 2
♣ 10 9 8 3

♠ A K Q 3
♡ A 8 2
♢ 10 8 7 3
♣ 7 4

West	North	East	South
–	1♣	Pass	1♠
2♢	2♠	Pass	4♠
All Pass			

A grand slam would be possible if trumps were 3–2 but North made a cautious rebid on the second round and the partnership stopped in game. It was enough. No, it was more than enough!

West began with a top diamond, ruffed in the dummy. Two rounds of trumps revealed the bad break and declarer then turned to the club suit. West was able to ruff the second round of clubs and he then led another diamond, removing the table's last trump. West ruffed the next round of clubs and the game went one down.

In only four spades declarer could easily afford to lose a trump trick. At trick two he should have ducked a trump. He could then win the return, draw trumps and run the club suit, making at least eleven tricks with ease.

South had a seemingly impregnable trump suit on the next hand, but he failed to play it to best advantage. The required move was simple in itself, but easy to miss.

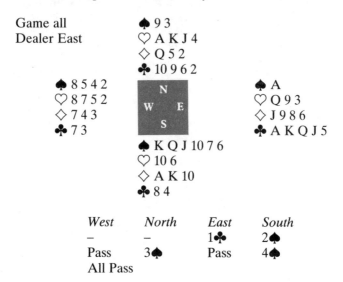

Game all
Dealer East

♠ 9 3
♡ A K J 4
♢ Q 5 2
♣ 10 9 6 2

♠ 8 5 4 2
♡ 8 7 5 2
♢ 7 4 3
♣ 7 3

♠ A
♡ Q 9 3
♢ J 9 8 6
♣ A K Q J 5

♠ K Q J 10 7 6
♡ 10 6
♢ A K 10
♣ 8 4

West	North	East	South
–	–	1♣	2♠
Pass	3♠	Pass	4♠
All Pass			

The defence started with three rounds of clubs and South ruffed with the king to prevent an overruff. He played a spade to the 9 and ace, and now a fourth club created a trick for West's 8 of trumps.

'Did you see that?' cried West jubilantly. 'My hand was 8-high, but I made the setting trick.'

'That was very clever of you,' observed North. Then, turning to his partner, 'Couldn't you have entered dummy with the ace of hearts and led ♠ 3 from the table?'

Trump coups

How can you take a trump finesse when you have a tenace in your hand but no trump to lead from the dummy? No, this isn't an insoluble Chinese riddle; it can be done, in an end position like this:

58

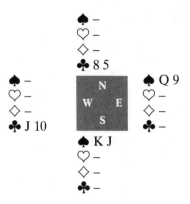

Spades are trumps and declarer scores the remaining tricks by leading a club from dummy.

The successful conclusion was possible only because declarer's trump length was the same as the defender's. Suppose instead that this had been the ending:

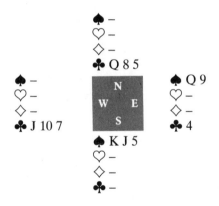

No good! Declarer will have to ruff the next club and will be in the wrong hand to pick up East's trumps.

Deliberately shortening your trumps to match those of the key defender is an important technique in preparing for a trump coup. Let's look at a complete deal where this is necessary.

North–South game
Dealer North

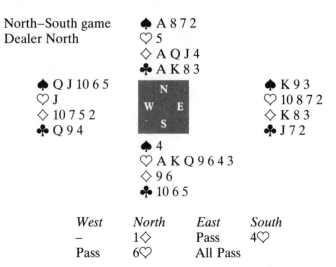

West	North	East	South
West	*North*	*East*	*South*
–	1♢	Pass	4♡
Pass	6♡	All Pass	

After a rough-hewn auction South arrives in six hearts. He wins the spade lead in dummy and sees that the slam is an excellent one. Twelve tricks will be there if trumps are 3–2 or if ♢ K is onside. A skilled practitioner will note an extra chance, that West will hold a singleton ♡ J or ♡ 10 and that a trump coup will be possible.

To realise this extra chance South will have to shorten his trumps to match the possible ♡ J x x x or ♡ 10 x x x in the East hand. At trick 2 he makes the apparently strange move of ruffing a spade. This proves to have been a wise investment when West plays the jack on the first round of hearts and shows out on the second.

A diamond finesse loses to the king and East returns a diamond. Declarer wins in dummy and cashes a third round of diamonds, throwing a club. He then ruffs a second spade, crosses to a top club and ruffs a third spade. South's trumps are now reduced to the same length as East's. When he returns to the dummy with a club this is the position:

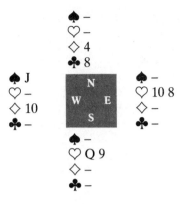

```
            ♠ –
            ♡ –
            ◇ 4
            ♣ 8
♠ J                      ♠ –
♡ –      [N]             ♡ 10 8
◇ 10   [W   E]          ◇ –
♣ –      [S]             ♣ –
            ♠ –
            ♡ Q 9
            ◇ –
            ♣ –
```

Declarer's earlier moves now bear fruit. He leads either of dummy's cards and scores his last two trumps.

Even when there is no element of a finesse declarer may be able to promote his own holding by leading a plain card towards it.

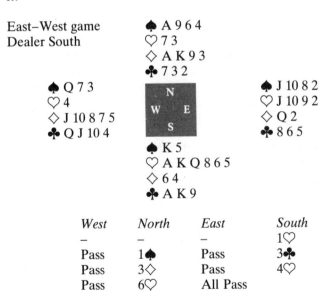

East–West game
Dealer South

```
                ♠ A 9 6 4
                ♡ 7 3
                ◇ A K 9 3
                ♣ 7 3 2
♠ Q 7 3                          ♠ J 10 8 2
♡ 4           [N]               ♡ J 10 9 2
◇ J 10 8 7 5  [W   E]           ◇ Q 2
♣ Q J 10 4    [S]               ♣ 8 6 5
                ♠ K 5
                ♡ A K Q 8 6 5
                ◇ 6 4
                ♣ A K 9
```

West	North	East	South
–	–	–	1♡
Pass	1♠	Pass	3♣
Pass	3◇	Pass	4♡
Pass	6♡	All Pass	

West starts with the queen of clubs, won in the South hand. Two rounds of trumps reveal a loser in that suit and it may seem that a club loser is unavoidable too. Look at it another way, though. Declarer has six winners outside the trump suit; if he can make all six trumps, this will bring his total to twelve.

At trick 4 declarer cashes the king of spades, followed by the ace of spades and a spade ruff. A diamond to dummy's ace allows another spade to be ruffed, East following all the while. After cashing his remaining club winner declarer crosses to the king of diamonds, leaving these cards still to be played:

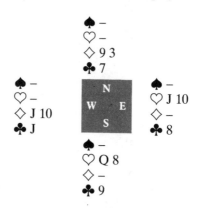

East has no answer to a diamond from the table. If he discards, declarer will score ♡ 8; if he ruffs, declarer will discard the losing club and claim the last two tricks. The ending would have been just as effective had declarer played off the queen of hearts earlier, retaining the singleton 8.

On the next deal declarer starts the play with similar intention, to make his own small trumps.

Game all   ♠ 3
Dealer North   ♡ A 7 4 2
              ♢ A Q 7 3
              ♣ A 10 6 5

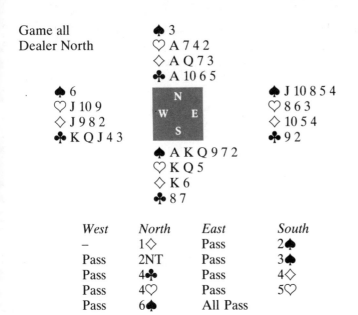

♠ 6   ♠ J 10 8 5 4
♡ J 10 9   ♡ 8 6 3
♢ J 9 8 2   ♢ 10 5 4
♣ K Q J 4 3   ♣ 9 2

                  ♠ A K Q 9 7 2
                  ♡ K Q 5
                  ♢ K 6
                  ♣ 8 7

West	North	East	South
–	1♢	Pass	2♠
Pass	2NT	Pass	3♠
Pass	4♣	Pass	4♢
Pass	4♡	Pass	5♡
Pass	6♠	All Pass	

Not an easy hand to bid, but South reaches the good contract of
six spades. He wins the king of clubs lead with the ace and cashes
two top trumps, no doubt wishing he hadn't bid the hand so well
when West shows out on the second round.

All is not quite lost. Declarer cashes three rounds of diamonds, disposing of his club loser, then shortens his trumps by
ruffing a club. He then stretches his luck to the limit by cashing
three rounds of hearts, finding East with precisely the 5–3–3–2
shape that was necessary. The lead is in dummy and these cards
remain:

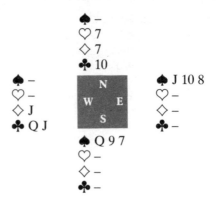

```
            ♠ –
            ♡ 7
            ◇ 7
            ♣ 10
  ♠ –           N        ♠ J 10 8
  ♡ –     W         E    ♡ –
  ◇ J                    ◇ –
  ♣ Q J         S        ♣ –
            ♠ Q 9 7
            ♡ –
            ◇ –
            ♣ –
```

'Any one you like,' declarer instructs his partner.

East must ruff high, to prevent declarer from scoring his 9, and South now underruffs! East is left on lead and must surrender the last two tricks.

Trump coups are possible also when the strong holding lies over you.

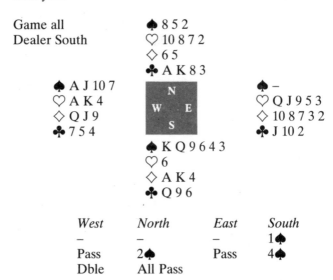

```
Game all              ♠ 8 5 2
Dealer South          ♡ 10 8 7 2
                      ◇ 6 5
                      ♣ A K 8 3
  ♠ A J 10 7     N        ♠ –
  ♡ A K 4   W         E   ♡ Q J 9 5 3
  ◇ Q J 9                 ◇ 10 8 7 3 2
  ♣ 7 5 4        S        ♣ J 10 2
                      ♠ K Q 9 6 4 3
                      ♡ 6
                      ◇ A K 4
                      ♣ Q 9 6
```

West	North	East	South
–	–	–	1♠
Pass	2♣	Pass	4♠
Dble	All Pass		

West started with two top hearts, declarer ruffing the second round. The king of trumps was taken by the ace, East showing out, and West switched to a club. Declarer cashed three rounds of clubs and the ace–king of diamonds. He then ruffed a diamond to arrive at this end position:

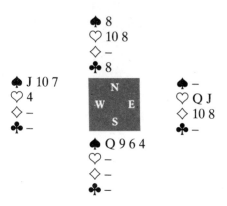

A heart is led and declarer ruffs with the 4, West following suit impotently. The final step is easy, a low spade from hand.

The smother play

There is one other type of 'impossible' trump finesse. Suppose that these trumps remain:

♠ A
♠ K 8   ♠ –
♠ Q J

Even the village idiot won't cover if you lead the queen, so how can you avoid losing a trick to West's king? The answer is to arrange for East to be on play, forced to lead a long card in a suit where the other three players are void. You ruff with the queen and West's king is guillotined.

As with the trump coups we saw a few moments ago, it is necessary for your own trump length at the finish to be the same as West's. On the deal below declarer has to take three ruffs to achieve this equality.

East–West game
Dealer South

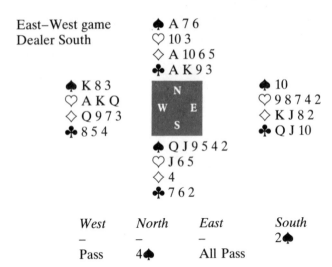

♠ A 7 6
♡ 10 3
◇ A 10 6 5
♣ A K 9 3

♠ K 8 3
♡ A K Q
◇ Q 9 7 3
♣ 8 5 4

♠ 10
♡ 9 8 7 4 2
◇ K J 8 2
♣ Q J 10

♠ Q J 9 5 4 2
♡ J 6 5
◇ 4
♣ 7 6 2

West	North	East	South
–	–	–	2♠
Pass	4♠	All Pass	

South opens with a skimpy weak two and is raised to game. West
cashes two high hearts and sees that a third high heart may
improve the life expectancy of his king of trumps.

Declarer ruffs the third round of hearts in the dummy, cashes
the diamond ace, and crosses to hand with a diamond ruff. The
queen of spades is run, dropping the 10 from East. Barring an
unlikely false card from East, it seems that West's king of trumps
must be guarded. Since there is an inescapable loser in clubs, and
two tricks have already been lost, prospects do not look too
bright.

It doesn't pay to give up at this game, though, and the wily
declarer crosses twice in clubs to take two more diamond ruffs.
This position has been reached:

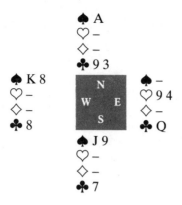

South exits with a club and, to his great good fortune, finds that East has to win the trick. The heart return spells doom to West's king of trumps.

5 How do the Cards Lie?

There are many clues to guide declarer as he gradually builds up
a picture of the opponents' hands. The earliest may come from
the defenders' bidding or, just as often, the lack of it.

Love all
Dealer West

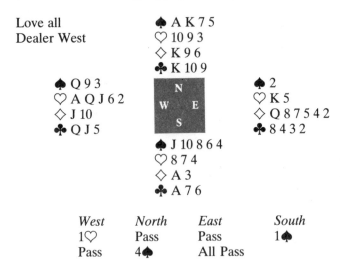

```
                    ♠ A K 7 5
                    ♡ 10 9 3
                    ◇ K 9 6
                    ♣ K 10 9
    ♠ Q 9 3              N              ♠ 2
    ♡ A Q J 6 2     W         E         ♡ K 5
    ◇ J 10               S              ◇ Q 8 7 5 4 2
    ♣ Q J 5                             ♣ 8 4 3 2
                    ♠ J 10 8 6 4
                    ♡ 8 7 4
                    ◇ A 3
                    ♣ A 7 6
```

West	North	East	South
1♡	Pass	Pass	1♠
Pass	4♠	All Pass	

North's raise to game was on the forward side, facing a protective
overcall. A cue bid of two hearts followed by a raise to three
spades would have sounded like three-and-a-half spades, express-
ing his values adequately.

Anyway, West leads ◇ J against the spade game. How much
does declarer know about the lie of the cards at this stage, do you
think? For a start, the opening lead places East with the diamond
queen. Also, since West would probably have started with a
heart had he held the ace–king, East is likely to hold one of the
top hearts, probably the king. Already you may reflect that if
East holds ♡ K and ◇ Q, West will hold the spade queen.

Fortified by this analysis, you win the diamond lead in your
own hand and run the jack of trumps. Two more rounds of

trumps are followed by the king of diamonds and a diamond ruff. When you cut loose with a heart the defenders take three rounds of the suit, leaving West on lead in this position:

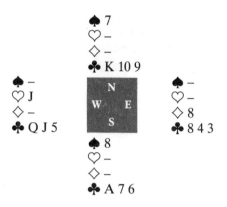

```
                    ♠ 7
                    ♡ –
                    ◇ –
                    ♣ K 10 9
    ♠ –                          ♠ –
    ♡ J            N             ♡ –
    ◇ –        W       E         ◇ 8
    ♣ Q J 5        S             ♣ 8 4 3
                    ♠ 8
                    ♡ –
                    ◇ –
                    ♣ A 7 6
```

West now exits with the queen of clubs. You are not tempted to play him for Q x x in the suit, since even the jack of clubs extra would have given East a likely response on the first round of bidding. You win the club queen with the ace and finesse successfully against the jack, making ten tricks.

'I had to give you four after passing,' says North smugly.

Safe or sorry?

Sometimes declarer needs to discover the lie of one suit in order to determine how to play another. This hand is a fairly simple example:

Love all ♠ A Q 4 3
Dealer North ♡ K 6 4
◇ K 5
♣ A 10 6 3

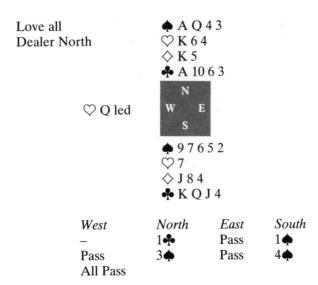

♡ Q led

♠ 9 7 6 5 2
♡ 7
◇ J 8 4
♣ K Q J 4

West	North	East	South
–	1♣	Pass	1♠
Pass	3♠	Pass	4♠
All Pass			

South reaches four spades and ruffs the second round of hearts. How should he continue?

The answer depends on whether he will need to make five tricks in spades or can afford to lose a trump trick. This is why the first play should be a diamond to the king. As the cards lie, the king wins. Let's look at the full hand:

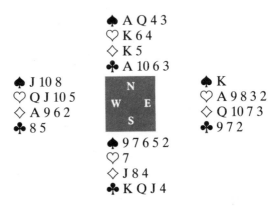

♠ A Q 4 3
♡ K 6 4
◇ K 5
♣ A 10 6 3

♠ J 10 8   ♠ K
♡ Q J 10 5   ♡ A 9 8 3 2
◇ A 9 6 2   ◇ Q 10 7 3
♣ 8 5   ♣ 9 7 2

♠ 9 7 6 5 2
♡ 7
◇ J 8 4
♣ K Q J 4

Knowing now that he can afford to lose one trump trick but not two, South makes the standard safety play of the ace. Now virtue is rewarded by the appearance of the king from East.

One extra point worth mentioning about the spade holding above: if South leads the first round from hand West should contribute the jack. This may incline South to think that the safety play will not be required.

Thinking backwards

Your estimate of how the cards lie in one suit will sometimes depend not on what you can see or discover in another suit, but on an assumption that you need to make. Let's look at this kind of problem in a miniature setting.

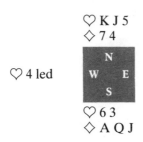

$\heartsuit$ K J 5
$\diamondsuit$ 7 4

$\heartsuit$ 4 led

$\heartsuit$ 6 3
$\diamondsuit$ A Q J

Towards the end of the play West leads $\heartsuit$ 4 through dummy's K J 5. The situation is that declarer can afford to lose only one more trick and must, therefore, assume that the diamond finesse will be right for him. It may follow from this, perhaps from East's silence during the bidding, that East is unlikely to hold $\heartsuit$ A as well as $\diamondsuit$ K. The logical play in hearts will then be to rise with dummy's king.

See how this type of thinking will solve a problem that arises quite early on the following deal:

Love all　　　　　　　 ♠ Q 8 7
Dealer East　　　　　　 ♡ Q 10 8
　　　　　　　　　　　 ◇ J 7 2
　　　　　　　　　　　 ♣ A Q 8 5

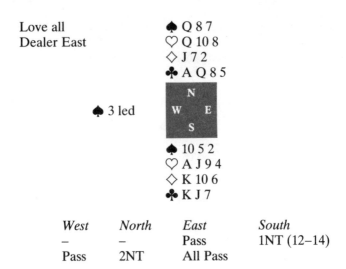

♠ 3 led

　　　　　　　　　　　 ♠ 10 5 2
　　　　　　　　　　　 ♡ A J 9 4
　　　　　　　　　　　 ◇ K 10 6
　　　　　　　　　　　 ♣ K J 7

West	*North*	*East*	*South*
–	–	Pass	1NT (12–14)
Pass	2NT	All Pass	

With such an ill-disposed 11-count North would be better advised to pass 1NT. He raises to 2NT, as players do, and West
leads a spade. Hoping that West's holding includes the jack of
spades, you play low from dummy at trick one. East wins with the
jack, cashes the ace, and after a little thought switches to a low
diamond. How will you play on this trick, and why?

Since the spades are presumably 4–3 there are five top losers –
four spades and the ace of diamonds. Is it an open guess how you
should play on this diamond lead?

No, because to have any chance for the contract you have to
assume that East holds ♡ K. Since he passed as dealer it is not
likely that he will hold ◇ A as well, since this would give him a
12-count. So you play West for the ace of diamonds and make the
contract when these are the defenders' hands:

　　　　　　♠ K 9 6 3　　　 ♠ A J 4
　　　　　　♡ 7 2　　　　　 ♡ K 6 5 3
　　　　　　◇ A 9 5　　　　 ◇ Q 8 4 3
　　　　　　♣ 9 6 4 3　　　 ♣ 10 2

The same type of reasoning will pay off on this hand:

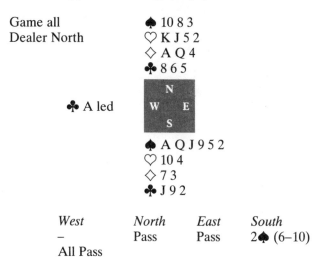

Game all · Dealer North

North:
♠ 10 8 3
♡ K J 5 2
♢ A Q 4
♣ 8 6 5

♣ A led

South:
♠ A Q J 9 5 2
♡ 10 4
♢ 7 3
♣ J 9 2

West	North	East	South
–	Pass	Pass	2♠ (6–10)
All Pass			

West, who leads the ace from ace–king, starts with ♣ A, drawing the 4 from his partner. He switches to ♢ 10 and without much hope you try the queen from dummy. East wins and plays queen and another club, won by West's king. West now switches to ♡ 6.

It is tempting to think: 'West has turned up with ♣ A K; it would be against the odds to place him with ♡ A; I'll put in the jack from dummy.'

There is a better way of analysing the situation. 'I have five certain losers already, so I must place East with the spade king. He is already marked with ♢ K J and ♣ Q. That's 9 points, so can he have ♡ A as well?'

Unlikely, since East did not open the bidding. The defending hands are:

♠ 7 4	♠ K 6
♡ A 8 6	♡ Q 9 7 3
♢ 10 9 6 2	♢ K J 8 5
♣ A K 10 7	♣ Q 4 3

and you must rise with dummy's king of hearts to make the contract.

A necessary assumption

In general, a declarer tends to think, what is the likely distribution? On some occasions he may need to ask himself a different question: what distribution do I *need* to find?

Game all
Dealer South

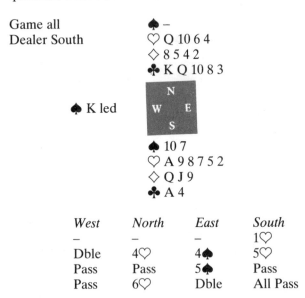

♠ –
♡ Q 10 6 4
◇ 8 5 4 2
♣ K Q 10 8 3

♠ K led

♠ 10 7
♡ A 9 8 7 5 2
◇ Q J 9
♣ A 4

West	North	East	South
–	–	–	1♡
Dble	4♡	4♠	5♡
Pass	Pass	5♠	Pass
Pass	6♡	Dble	All Pass

The doubtful bid in this auction is North's six hearts. Apart from the fact that a player who has pre-empted should seldom bid again, North's clubs, sitting over the player who has doubled, look to be a strong defensive holding.

West led the king of spades and dummy ruffed. South led a heart to the ace, East following suit and West dropping the jack. The second round of spades was ruffed and South came back to hand with a club to the ace. What should he do now?

To find a 3–3 club break will not assist declarer. Someone, no doubt West, will ruff the fourth round of clubs and South will still have one diamond left. The only chance is to score *four* club tricks before the defenders can ruff. For this to be possible West must hold ♡ K and either ♣ J x x x or ♣ x x x x (you must guess which). If West has four clubs to his partner's two he is twice as likely to hold the jack. So, ace of clubs and a club to the 10 is the best line of play.

South followed this line in a Crockford's match many years ago, and this turned out to be the full hand:

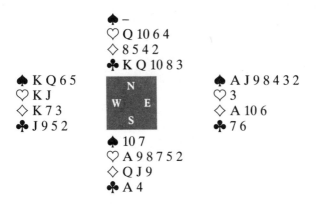

```
            ♠ –
            ♡ Q 10 6 4
            ◇ 8 5 4 2
            ♣ K Q 10 8 3
♠ K Q 6 5                        ♠ A J 9 8 4 3 2
♡ K J            N               ♡ 3
◇ K 7 3      W       E           ◇ A 10 6
♣ J 9 5 2        S               ♣ 7 6
            ♠ 10 7
            ♡ A 9 8 7 5 2
            ◇ Q J 9
            ♣ A 4
```

As you may imagine, East wasn't pleased when he saw declarer discard three diamonds on dummy's clubs and then claim the contract. 'What's the use of leading a spade?' he demanded.

That was a bit unfair. West has a sure trump trick and his partner has doubled, so it is reasonable for him to make a safe lead that cannot cost a trick.

Find the lady

We all play in many contracts that depend on a queen finesse. South, on the next deal, was missing four trumps to the queen and could not afford to lose a trump trick. He found a novel solution to his problem.

Love all
Dealer West

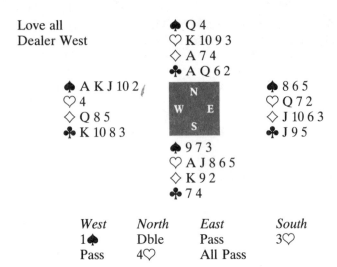

	♠ Q 4	
	♡ K 10 9 3	
	◇ A 7 4	
	♣ A Q 6 2	

♠ A K J 10 2
♡ 4
◇ Q 8 5
♣ K 10 8 3

♠ 8 6 5
♡ Q 7 2
◇ J 10 6 3
♣ J 9 5

♠ 9 7 3
♡ A J 8 6 5
◇ K 9 2
♣ 7 4

West	North	East	South
1♣	Dble	Pass	3♡
Pass	4♡	All Pass	

West played three rounds of spades, South ruffing the third round with dummy's ♡ 9. The contract depended on locating the trump queen, but declarer was in no hurry to play on trumps. He came to hand with the king of diamonds and took a successful club finesse. After ace of clubs and a club ruff, West dropping the king from his equals, declarer crossed to dummy's ace of diamonds, reaching this end position:

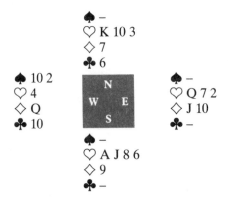

	♠ –	
	♡ K 10 3	
	◇ 7	
	♣ 6	

♠ 10 2
♡ 4
◇ Q
♣ 10

♠ –
♡ Q 7 2
◇ J 10
♣ –

♠ –
♡ A J 8 6
◇ 9
♣ –

When dummy's last club was played, East discarded. Declarer could now ruff low and exit in diamonds; the contract was assured wherever the trump queen lay. Had East produced the last club, declarer would have been forced to take a view of the trump suit on that trick. He would be in no worse a position, though, than if he had tried to guess the trumps earlier in the play.

There is a general assumption, expressed in many books, that the declarer should draw trumps unless there is a clear reason not to (a desire to ruff, usually). If you watch good players, though, you will find that they often delay until they know a little about the general distribution.

Can you count?

We have now arrived at the most important technique used to reconstruct the opponents' hands – counting. The main difference between good players and the rest is that good players constantly strive to obtain a count of the hand, in terms of both high cards and distribution. You cannot form a better habit!

East–West game
Dealer South

♠ 8 4 2
♡ 10 3
◇ K 10 4 2
♣ K 6 4 3

♠ 6 5
♡ A 9 8 6 5 2
◇ 5
♣ J 10 8 7

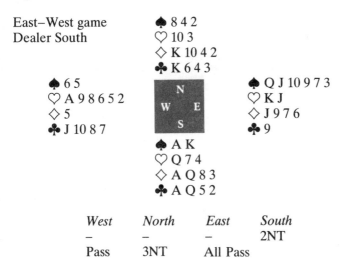

♠ Q J 10 9 7 3
♡ K J
◇ J 9 7 6
♣ 9

♠ A K
♡ Q 7 4
◇ A Q 8 3
♣ A Q 5 2

West	North	East	South
–	–	–	2NT
Pass	3NT	All Pass	

West leads ♡ 6 and East wins with the king. (If East was likely to regain the lead, it might be good play for him to try the *jack*. If South accepted the bait and won with the queen, the route back to West's hand would be clear.) East thinks about returning a spade, but rightly assesses the jack of hearts as a better prospect.

Not suspecting East of having played a clever game with A K J x x, you play low and are happy to see East switch to the queen of spades.

Prospects of nine tricks seem good now, but when you cash the ace and queen of clubs East shows out. If you are alert you will count West for six hearts and four clubs. When he follows to a second round of spades he is known to hold at most one diamond. So, you cross to the king of diamonds and lead the 10 from dummy, intending to run it; if East covers with the jack you can return to dummy with the king of clubs for a finesse of ♢ Q 8. Simple, but the mark of an expert player.

Keep counting

Are you still counting? It will help on the next deal, too.

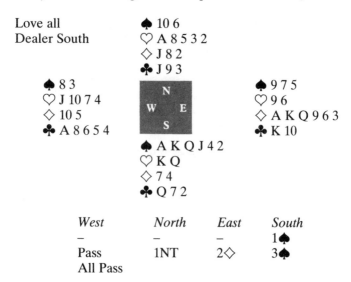

Love all — ♠ 10 6
Dealer South — ♡ A 8 5 3 2
♢ J 8 2
♣ J 9 3

♠ 8 3
♡ J 10 7 4
♢ 10 5
♣ A 8 6 5 4

♠ 9 7 5
♡ 9 6
♢ A K Q 9 6 3
♣ K 10

♠ A K Q J 4 2
♡ K Q
♢ 7 4
♣ Q 7 2

West	North	East	South
–	–	–	1♠
Pass	1NT	2♢	3♠
All Pass			

Some players would pass on the East cards, hoping to find themselves on lead against a (preferably high) no-trump contract. You pays your money and you takes your choice. Whenever South rebids in one of the majors you will wish you had introduced the diamonds.

Anyway, West leads ♢ 10 against three spades and East plays off the ace, king and queen. You ruff high on the third round and

West discards a club. After cashing ♡ K Q, you play ace of spades and a spade to the 10, all following. All will be well if the heart ace stands up, but East ruffs with the outstanding trump. You overruff and survey the North–South cards in the following end position:

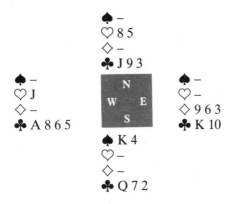

Most players, having already lost two diamonds, would now try a finesse of ♣ 9; but this is the equivalent of playing with your eyes shut. East has already turned up with three spades, two hearts, and six diamonds; he is therefore marked with a doubleton club, probably A x or K x.

Your best move at this point is the *queen* of clubs. If East wins the trick you will follow with a club to the jack on the next round. If instead West wins the first club you will finesse the 9 on the next round. Playing in this fashion you don't lose the contract when East holds ♣ A 10 or ♣ K 10.

6 Department of Clever Tricks

Bridge would be a dull game if it were just a matter of technical expertise. The object of this chapter is not to enumerate the standard, well-known, types of deception within a single suit; it is more to describe a variety of moves, quite simple in themselves, that may cause the opposition to do the wrong thing.

What, for example, could be simpler than the play of the following hand?

Love all
Dealer North

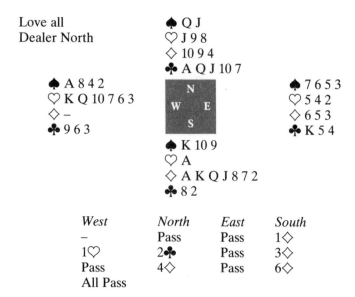

| ♠ Q J |
| ♡ J 9 8 |
| ◇ 10 9 4 |
| ♣ A Q J 10 7 |

♠ A 8 4 2
♡ K Q 10 7 6 3
◇ –
♣ 9 6 3

♠ 7 6 5 3
♡ 5 4 2
◇ 6 5 3
♣ K 5 4

♠ K 10 9
♡ A
◇ A K Q J 8 7 2
♣ 8 2

West	North	East	South
–	Pass	Pass	1◇
1♡	2♣	Pass	3◇
Pass	4◇	Pass	6◇
All Pass			

West leads the king of hearts to your ace. What would you do now? The contract is going to depend on the club finesse, apparently, so perhaps you would draw trumps and lead a club to the queen. If the clubs go well you may even make seven, discarding three spades on dummy's clubs.

But meanwhile West will have signalled heavily in spades. When East comes in with the king of clubs he will hearken to His Master's Voice and you will be one down.

It is important, therefore, to give East his chance in clubs *before West has had a chance to signal*. So, lead ♣ 8 at trick two and put in the queen. Sometimes it might be clever for East to hold off, but not on this occasion. And if he wins, is it not quite possible that he will return a heart? His partner could easily have only five hearts and no ace of spades.

True, East might ask himself why you are playing a club, not a trump, at this early stage. But, then again, he may not.

On the next deal the opponents find your weakness with their opening lead. You are in six spades and we present the deal in problem form.

Game all
Dealer South

♠ J 10 6 5 4
♡ A J 7 5
♢ –
♣ 9 8 4 2

♣ Q led

♠ K Q 8 7 3
♡ Q
♢ A K Q 5 4
♣ A 7

West	North	East	South
–	–	–	1♠
Pass	4♣	Pass	4NT
Pass	6♢ (1)	Pass	6♠
All Pass			

(1) One ace and a void in the bid suit (diamonds)

You win the club lead with the ace and must dispose of your club loser before playing on trumps. What is the best shot, do you think – to take a heart finesse or to play for three discards on the diamonds?

Since the chance of three diamonds standing up is roughly 80%, against 50% for the heart finesse, it is perhaps tempting to bang out the ace, king and queen of diamonds. In some cases, though, this will be the end of the story. For example:

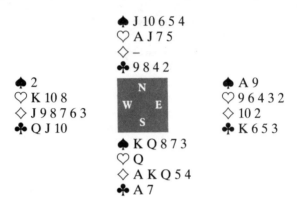

♠ J 10 6 5 4
♡ A J 7 5
◇ —
♣ 9 8 4 2

♠ 2
♡ K 10 8
◇ J 9 8 7 6 3
♣ Q J 10

♠ A 9
♡ 9 6 4 3 2
◇ 10 2
♣ K 6 5 3

♠ K Q 8 7 3
♡ Q
◇ A K Q 5 4
♣ A 7

'Can you believe it?' South may exclaim when the third diamond is ruffed. 'The heart finesse was right all the time!'

Yes, unlucky to find the diamonds 6–2, but what about leading the queen of hearts at trick two? Not many players in the West chair would play low without a qualm. And of course, if West does play low South will overtake, ruff a heart, and play for the superior chance in diamonds. At least he will have tried!

Concealing your strength

Defenders are always more likely to go wrong if put to the key decision early in the play, when little evidence is available. Sometimes you will even have an opportunity to 'doctor' the evidence before them. Try the next hand in 3NT.

Game all   ♠ Q 4
Dealer South   ♡ 8 5
                   ◇ A J 10 8
                   ♣ J 10 8 4 2

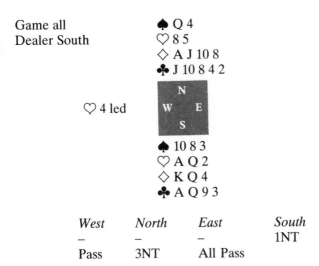

♡ 4 led

                   ♠ 10 8 3
                   ♡ A Q 2
                   ◇ K Q 4
                   ♣ A Q 9 3

West	*North*	*East*	*South*
–	–	–	1NT
Pass	3NT	All Pass	

West leads a heart against 3NT and East plays the jack. Lucky they didn't reel off five spade tricks, you think, as you win with the queen.

Did you win with the queen? What about that resolve always to take your time before playing from dummy at trick one?

This contract, after the lead, is always going to be made easily if the club finesse is right; if it is wrong, you are likely to lose a club and at least four spades. If West can place you with ♡ A Q, he will surely try a spade when he comes in. So?

The jack of hearts was a card you should have been pleased to see. If you win with the *ace* it will look to West as though his partner holds the queen of hearts as well as the jack; he may well persist with hearts when he comes in with the club king. Suppose the full hand is something like this:

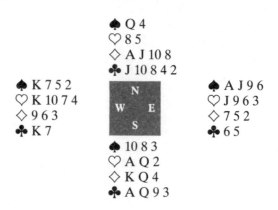

                    ♠ Q 4
                    ♡ 8 5
                    ◇ A J 10 8
                    ♣ J 10 8 4 2
    ♠ K 7 5 2   ♠ A J 9 6
    ♡ K 10 7 4   ♡ J 9 6 3
    ◇ 9 6 3   ◇ 7 5 2
    ♣ K 7   ♣ 6 5
                    ♠ 10 8 3
                    ♡ A Q 2
                    ◇ K Q 4
                    ♣ A Q 9 3

You make the recommended play of winning the heart lead with
the ace, cross to the diamond ace, and run the jack of clubs to
West's king. If he finds a spade switch now . . . congratulate him.

The following hand is a first cousin to the last one, but
declarer's best play is even less likely to be recognised by the
defenders.

North–South game   ♠ 6
Dealer South   ♡ 10 5 2
                         ◇ J 10 8 4 3
                         ♣ K 10 9 3
    ♠ A Q 8 7 3   ♠ 10 5 4 2
    ♡ Q 8 6   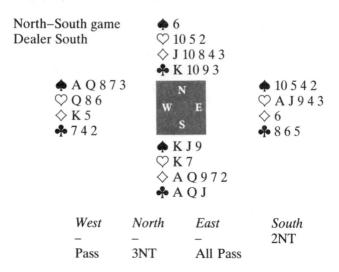   ♡ A J 9 4 3
    ◇ K 5   ◇ 6
    ♣ 7 4 2   ♣ 8 6 5
                         ♠ K J 9
                         ♡ K 7
                         ◇ A Q 9 7 2
                         ♣ A Q J

West	North	East	South
–	–	–	2NT
Pass	3NT	All Pass	

West leads ♠ 7 and you should win East's 10 with the king! Then
you cross to dummy in clubs and run the jack of diamonds to

West's king. While some defenders are prepared for the play described on the preceding hand – the ace from A Q x – they tend not to think of the possibility of king from K J x. In all probability West will win the diamond and lead a low spade to his partner's imagined jack. (To play his spades from the top would give declarer a second stop when he had started with K 9 x x).

If instead you win the first trick with the jack of spades, then West will surely switch to ♡ 8 when he comes in. Alerted by the *high* heart that West is not looking for tricks in that suit, East will switch back to spades.

Note that in both the last two examples the deception will work only if the card that the declarer is concealing is one that the third player might logically have held. Thus, when ♠ 10 is headed by the king, it will seem to West that his partner holds J 10. The card that is concealed will usually be just one range higher than the card played by the defender.

Sometimes you have to conceal weakness, rather than strength. How would you tackle this one?

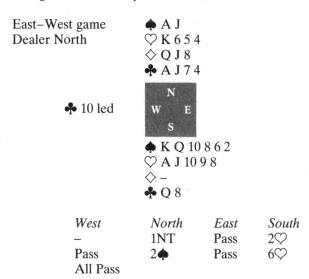

		♠ A J	
East–West game		♡ K 6 5 4	
Dealer North		◇ Q J 8	
		♣ A J 7 4	

♣ 10 led

♠ K Q 10 8 6 2
♡ A J 10 9 8
◇ –
♣ Q 8

West	North	East	South
–	1NT	Pass	2♡
Pass	2♠	Pass	6♡
All Pass			

It is not our style of bidding but South jumps straight to the six level, hoping to put West to a difficult lead. Annoyingly, West still finds a club lead, the 10. Any ideas on how the hand should be played?

To begin with, the club finesse is unlikely to be right. If you let the club run you will be dependent on not losing a trump trick. The way to give yourself an extra chance is to go up with the ace of clubs, dropping the queen from hand, then play king and another heart. If East shows out, let West win with the queen (having seen only one discard from his partner). If instead East follows to the second round with another low card, finesse the jack. You win when East holds three trumps to the queen, also perhaps when this is the distribution:

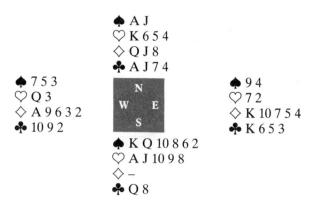

```
                ♠ A J
                ♡ K 6 5 4
                ◇ Q J 8
                ♣ A J 7 4
    ♠ 7 5 3                           ♠ 9 4
    ♡ Q 3            N                ♡ 7 2
    ◇ A 9 6 3 2   W     E             ◇ K 10 7 5 4
    ♣ 10 9 2         S                ♣ K 6 5 3
                ♠ K Q 10 8 6 2
                ♡ A J 10 9 8
                ◇ –
                ♣ Q 8
```

When West comes in with the queen of hearts it is at any rate possible that he will try a diamond rather than a club. Dummy's clubs will then be parked on your splendid spade suit. In terms of probability, by the way, you lose very little by finessing in hearts on the second round.

The play could be just as effective if you took the heart finesse the other way, ace first and run the jack. East would be reluctant to cash his king of clubs in case the opening lead was from 10 9 8 x; declarer might have 6–5–1–1 shape with a losing single-ton in diamonds.

The next hand offers a good chance for deception, too – the more so if you *always* take your time before playing any card to the first trick. (Did we mention that before? Sorry!)

East–West game
Dealer South

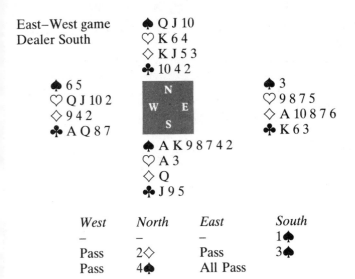

♠ Q J 10
♡ K 6 4
◇ K J 5 3
♣ 10 4 2

♠ 6 5
♡ Q J 10 2
◇ 9 4 2
♣ A Q 8 7

♠ 3
♡ 9 8 7 5
◇ A 10 8 7 6
♣ K 6 3

♠ A K 9 8 7 4 2
♡ A 3
◇ Q
♣ J 9 5

West	North	East	South
–	–	–	1♠
Pass	2◇	Pass	3♠
Pass	4♠	All Pass	

West leads the queen of hearts and you have an early vision of one down – no way to avoid four losers. Don't despair. *Play low from both hands on the first trick.* There is a very good chance that West will continue with the jack of hearts. Then, after two rounds of trumps, you discard the queen of diamonds on the king of hearts and lead the king of diamonds through East, establishing a discard for one of your club losers. Also, you may create some discord between your opponents!

Two knavish tricks

Now that you have the general idea, see how you cope with two more difficult problems. On the first one you are in 3NT.

Love all   ♠ 5 2
Dealer South   ♡ A Q 8 4
                ◇ K 9 3 2
                ♣ 9 7 2

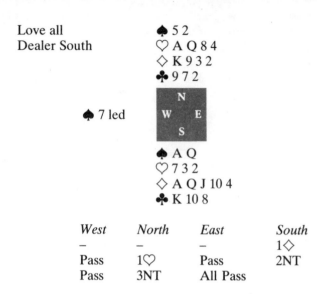

♠ 7 led

♠ A Q
♡ 7 3 2
◇ A Q J 10 4
♣ K 10 8

West	North	East	South
–	–	–	1◇
Pass	1♡	Pass	2NT
Pass	3NT	All Pass	

With a chunky five-card suit and two tens you rebid 2NT rather than 1NT. The man opposite raises to game and the spade lead goes to East's king and your ace.

What would you do now? You have eight tricks on top and maybe five rounds of diamonds will inconvenience the defenders. But not if the cards lie:

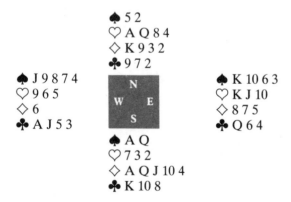

                ♠ 5 2
                ♡ A Q 8 4
                ◇ K 9 3 2
                ♣ 9 7 2

♠ J 9 8 7 4   ♠ K 10 6 3
♡ 9 6 5   ♡ K J 10
◇ 6   ◇ 8 7 5
♣ A J 5 3   ♣ Q 6 4

                ♠ A Q
                ♡ 7 3 2
                ◇ A Q J 10 4
                ♣ K 10 8

When South plays off the diamonds West will part with two hearts and two clubs, East with one spade and one club. As soon as the defenders come in they will clear the spades and South will have nowhere to go for his ninth trick.

We don't say this would be poor play by the declarer, but did you think of entering dummy with a diamond and leading a club to the king at trick three? This type of deception will very seldom cost. In fact, it will gain more often against strong opponents than weak ones. West, not knowing that South has five tricks in diamonds, *may well hold off* the king of clubs – usually good play when declarer leads towards what looks like a king–queen holding. If, at worst, the king is headed by the ace the defenders are not likely to take five tricks in the suit; the heart finesse will still be available.

You may think that the early lead to the king of clubs was a bit tricky. Bear it in mind, though, as you look at the next hand. It is pairs scoring, where overtricks are worth their weight in match points, if not in gold.

Love all
Dealer South

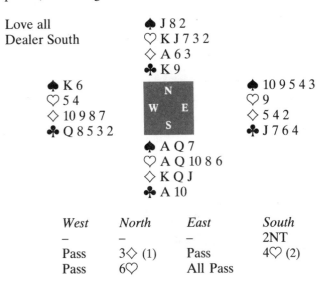

♠ J 8 2
♡ K J 7 3 2
♢ A 6 3
♣ K 9

♠ K 6
♡ 5 4
♢ 10 9 8 7
♣ Q 8 5 3 2

♠ 10 9 5 4 3
♡ 9
♢ 5 4 2
♣ J 7 6 4

♠ A Q 7
♡ A Q 10 8 6
♢ K Q J
♣ A 10

West	North	East	South
–	–	–	2NT
Pass	3♢ (1)	Pass	4♡ (2)
Pass	6♡	All Pass	

(1) Transfer bid, indicating hearts
(2) Indicating a maximum with a good fit

When South opens 2NT (the best call on his hand) there is a good case for North to raise straight to 6NT. Twelve, but only twelve, tricks would be straightforward in that contract. Let's suppose that you reach six hearts instead, and West leads ◇ 10.

The identical shape of the North and South hands is not a good omen. Unless you can conjure an overtrick the pairs who manoeuvre into 6NT will outscore you. The best you can do is to play off some winners, arriving at this position with the lead in dummy:

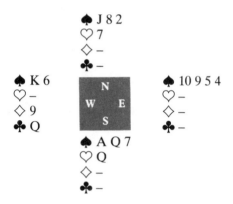

              ♠ J 8 2
              ♡ 7
              ◇ –
              ♣ –

♠ K 6   ♠ 10 9 5 4
♡ –   ♡ –
◇ 9   ◇ –
♣ Q   ♣ –

              ♠ A Q 7
              ♡ Q
              ◇ –
              ♣ –

Since East discarded a spade early on it is inconceivable that he is now holding a doubleton king of spades. A finesse of the spade queen cannot therefore yield an overtrick. There are two other possible plays, either of which might succeed when West holds the doubleton king.

You could lead the ace of spades from hand! West may well place his partner with Q 10 x and unblock the king, hoping to avoid an end-play. Another chance is to lead low towards the table. If West places you with A 10 x he will smoothly play low, trusting you to finesse on the next round, after the jack has lost to East's presumed queen. In fact dummy's jack will win and you, equally smoothly, will play a spade to the ace, dropping West's king.

Don't fail to look for these 'impossible' plays when you are desperate for an extra trick. That fact that your play is 'impossible' will often puzzle an opponent, trapping him into playing an 'impossible' defence.

7 Choosing the Right Line

Choosing between different lines of play can be a tricky business. On some hands you will need a general idea of the odds affecting various distributions. On others you may have to engage in some detective work before making a critical decision; for example, discovering which defender has the longer heart holding before guessing where the queen of that suit lies. There will also be occasions where you choose a particular line simply because, if it fails, it may give the defenders more chance to err.

In this chapter we present various deals in problem form. Some of them will involve themes that we have touched upon in the previous chapters.

Legend of the 3–3 break

Most players, even if not interested in odds, know that a finesse is a better prospect than playing for a 3–3 break. Circumstances alter cases, though. Have a look at this deal.

Love all   ♠ K 10 9 7
Dealer North   ♡ A K 8 7 2
                 ◇ 10 2
                 ♣ Q 10

♣ 9 led

                 ♠ A Q J 8 6 4
                 ♡ 6 5
                 ◇ A Q J
                 ♣ K J

West	North	East	South
–	1♡	Pass	2♠
Pass	4♠ (1)	Pass	4NT (2)
Pass	5♡ (3)	Pass	6♠
All Pass			

(1) Good support but minimum hand
(2) Roman Key-Card Blackwood
(3) Two of the five 'aces' (♠ K counting as an ace)

A club is led against six spades. East wins with the ace and fires back a middling diamond, the 6. What would you do?

You could finesse the queen of diamonds or you could go up with the ace, playing for hearts to be 3–3 and to provide two discards. The books will tell you that the odds of a finesse succeeding are 50%, of a 3–3 break 36%. You may be surprised when we say that there is a powerful reason to play for the even break on this particular hand.

If West had held low diamonds as well as low clubs he might equally well have led a diamond, so there is a presumption that his holding in diamonds is different. In effect, there has been almost a halving of the odds that the diamond finesse is right, making the finesse not much more than 25% against the 36% for the even heart break.

Nor, for that matter, do we believe the 36% figure for the 3–3 break. When there has been no enemy action during the bidding, many of the uneven distributions are more or less excluded. That makes the normal divisions much more likely. (On hands where the opponents have between them the values to compete, but choose not to, the initial chance of a 3–3 break in one of your side suits may be not far short of 50%).

When this deal actually arose, in an old England–Scotland match, any such reasoning escaped the declarer. He took a losing finesse in diamonds and found that hearts had been 3–3.

Choice of three

On the next deal the contract is 6NT and there are at least three possible lines of play.

East–West game
Dealer South

♠ J 3
♡ 6 5 4
♢ Q J 10 8 5
♣ A 10 2

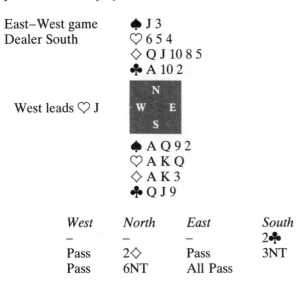

West leads ♡ J

♠ A Q 9 2
♡ A K Q
♢ A K 3
♣ Q J 9

West	North	East	South
–	–	–	2♣
Pass	2♢	Pass	3NT
Pass	6NT	All Pass	

West's lead is unhelpful and you can count only ten tricks on top. What do you think is the best line?

A winning club finesse would see you home at once, and if it failed you would still have the spade finesse as a second chance. This line gives you odds of approximately 3 to 1 on. Alternatively, you might run a few diamonds and follow with the jack of spades. If this finesse wins you can turn to the clubs, but if it loses and West switches to a club, as he probably will, you will have to decide whether to take the club finesse or hope for a third trick from the spade suit, slightly against the odds.

Perhaps you are there now? The best way to retain all the chances is to lead a low spade to the jack at trick two. If West goes in with the king you will have twelve tricks, and if the jack of spades holds you will finesse in clubs for an overtrick. What if the jack loses to East's king, though? You will now be able to test the spades, trying to drop the 10 in three rounds, before reverting to the club finesse. Playing in this fashion you are about 6 to 1 on to make the slam.

Look for the clue

You're still at the helm and on this occasion the opponents provide you with a little help by taking their tricks early on.

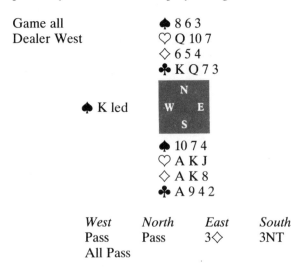

Game all   ♠ 8 6 3
Dealer West   ♡ Q 10 7
                ◇ 6 5 4
                ♣ K Q 7 3

♠ K led

♠ 10 7 4
♡ A K J
◇ A K 8
♣ A 9 4 2

West	North	East	South
Pass	Pass	3◇	3NT
All Pass			

West leads the king of spades and by good fortune the suit turns out to be 4–3, East holding A 9 2. On the fourth spade East discards a diamond. You throw a diamond from dummy and the king of hearts from hand.

West now exits with a heart, which runs to your ace. There is no possibility of finding East (who opened 3◇) with four clubs, that's for sure. They might be 3–2 or, come to think of it, you would have chances if East held a singleton 8, 10 or jack.

It can't be wrong to lay down the ace of clubs. East drops the 8, which is encouraging. But if you follow with the 9 of clubs and West, in sphinx-like fashion, plays low, are you going to let the 9 run or not?

Of course, you don't want to answer that question, and there is no reason why you should. Just play off two more hearts, followed by the ace of diamonds, discovering that East's shape is 3–2–7–1. Then you lead the 9 of clubs, confidently letting it run if West plays low. (If West covers you can return to ♢ K to repeat the finesse).

East's hand was:

♠ A 9 2　　♡ 4 3　　♢ Q J 10 9 7 3 2　　♣ 8

More detective work

This deal has an element in common with the last – you investigate one suit to assist you in your play of another. Unearthing a clue is one thing, though, the correct deduction may still elude you.

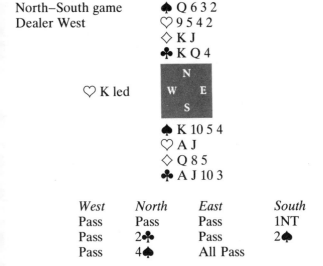

North–South game
Dealer West

♠ Q 6 3 2
♡ 9 5 4 2
♢ K J
♣ K Q 4

♡ K led

♠ K 10 5 4
♡ A J
♢ Q 8 5
♣ A J 10 3

West	North	East	South
Pass	Pass	Pass	1NT
Pass	2♣	Pass	2♠
Pass	4♠	All Pass	

West attacks with the king of hearts and you win in the South hand. Everything depends on picking up the trumps for only one loser and the normal play would be low to the queen, followed by a finesse of the 10.

Suppose you test the diamond suit first, though, and find that West has the ace. Since West failed to open the bidding, East must hold the ace of spades. Does that change your play in the trump suit? Think about it for a few moments before reading on.

Indeed it should change your play. If you can place the ace with East your first play should be low to the king. If the king wins you duck on the next round (unless the jack shows from West).

You may be surprised to hear that this is a better play. To check, count the situations where each play gains over the other. Low to the king, and low on the way back, gains when East holds A 9, A 8, A 7, A 9 8, A 9 7, A 8 7. The alternative, starting with low to the queen, gains when East holds A J 9, A J 8, A J 7. Six to three in favour of the recommended play.

When breaks are bad

The next deal looks at first glance like a fairly simple elimination. In fact, if both black suits are unkind you must find a precise sequence of plays to land the contract.

Love all   ♠ A J 8 7
Dealer South   ♡ A K
                  ♦ 10 8 4
                  ♣ K Q 7 6

♠ 5 led
```
        N
      W   E
        S
```

                  ♠ K Q 10 6 2
                  ♡ –
                  ♦ A J 9 7 3
                  ♣ A 8 2

West	North	East	South
–	–	–	1♠
Pass	2NT (1)	Pass	3♦
Pass	4♠ (2)	Pass	6♠
All Pass			

(1) Baron 2NT, 16+ points and a balanced hand
(2) Lower-range Baron bid with 4-card trump
    support

East follows to the first round of trumps. What now? You would
like to eliminate hearts and clubs, then run a diamond to West,
leaving him end-played. Suppose you begin blithely by drawing
trumps, finding them 3–1. If West then turns up with four or
more clubs, you will end in the South hand after ruffing dummy's
fourth club. There will be no convenient entry back to table to
lead a diamond.

On the actual deal West had one trump, five clubs, and (of
course) ♦ K Q x. Can the contract still be made, do you think?

The winning play is to capture the trump lead in hand, cash the
ace of clubs, and return to dummy with a second round of
trumps. You then cash the two heart winners, throwing clubs,
and ruff a club. After returning to dummy with a third round of
trumps, you cash the king and queen of clubs. At this stage you
have one trump in each hand and ♦ 10 8 4 opposite ♦ A J 9. You
play a diamond to the jack, claiming the remainder.

West's hand was:

    ♠ 5   ♡ J 9 8 6   ♦ K Q 6   ♣ J 9 5 4 3

As you see, you had to walk a tightrope to make the contract. Any wayward step and you would tumble to defeat.

Still on the same theme, foreseeing and countering bad breaks, try this one. West's 4♡ overcall tells you that the breaks will not be kind.

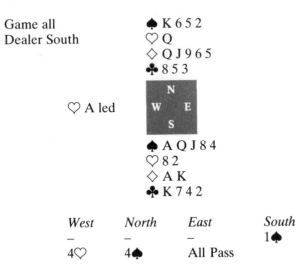

Game all
Dealer South

♠ K 6 5 2
♡ Q
♢ Q J 9 6 5
♣ 8 5 3

♡ A led

♠ A Q J 8 4
♡ 8 2
♢ A K
♣ K 7 4 2

West	North	East	South
–	–	–	1♠
4♡	4♠	All Pass	

West leads the ace of hearts and continues with the king. What division of the cards will put your contract at risk?

Suppose that, after ruffing the second heart, you play a trump to the South hand. A calamity occurs! West shows out on the first round of trumps. Dummy has one trump fewer than East, so you will not be able to draw trumps before running dummy's diamonds. The best you can do is to unblock ♢ A K, cross to the king of trumps, and hope to cash two more diamonds before East can ruff. No good. These were the defenders' hands:

West	East
♠ –	♠ 10 9 7 3
♡ A K 9 7 6 4 3	♡ J 10 5
♢ 7 4 2	♢ 10 8 3
♣ A J 6	♣ Q 10 9

East will ruff the fourth diamond, leaving you a trick short.

You have seen what went wrong? At trick 2 you should have let West's $\heartsuit$ K hold the trick. He can do you no damage with his next lead (if he had a singleton club, he would surely have switched to it at trick 2). You can then play one round of trumps, unblock the diamonds, and play three more rounds of trumps, ending in the dummy.

There is nothing at all difficult in making such a play, provided you always take time at the beginning of a hand to ask yourself: what can go wrong here?

Did you notice something else about the hand? West missed the chance of a clever play at trick 2. If he continues with a *low* heart, instead of the king, declarer will be forced to ruff to prevent East gaining the lead and sending a club through. Let him try to make the contract now.

Averting an overruff

Sometimes, when you would like to ruff a suit in dummy, there is reason to fear an overruff. Can anything be done to reduce the risk? Well, one possibility is to look for your ruff in a different suit.

Game all   ♠ 7 6
Dealer West   ♡ Q 10 2
                    ◇ 10 8 7 4 3
                    ♣ K 7 4

♠ K led

                    ♠ A 8 3
                    ♡ A K 7 5 4 3
                    ◇ A
                    ♣ Q 8 5

West	North	East	South
2♠	Pass	Pass	Dble (1)
Pass	3◇	Pass	3♡
Pass	4♡	All Pass	

(1) South is too strong for 3♡, which he would
     bid on an ace less. Also, if partner has a
     good club suit a high club contract may be
     possible

You can see nine easy tricks and a spade ruff would bring the
total to ten. However, West's opening bid marks East with a
likely doubleton in spades. How can you prevent an overruff?

If you ruff the third spade with the queen you will lose a
subsequent trump trick unless trumps are 2–2, or the jack is
singleton. You might try ruffing with the 10, but East, with two
spades to his partner's six, is favourite to hold the heart jack. In
any case, there is a much better line available.

You should duck the first spade, win the second, and play a
club to the king and ace. After winning the return you play a third
round of spades, throwing a club from dummy. Now you draw
two rounds of trumps and play to ruff a club in dummy. This line
will succeed provided East has at least four clubs (three is no
good, because he can throw one on the third round of spades).
By 'trading ruffs', as it is called, you substantially improve your
chances.

Second string to the bow

The original declarer on the next hand chose the wrong line. Why? Very likely because he thought there was only one line.

Game all
Dealer South

♠ 10 2
♡ K 9 7 4 2
♢ 6
♣ A 10 7 6 2

♢ Q led

```
      N
  W       E
      S
```

♠ A K Q J 9 8
♡ A
♢ A K
♣ 8 5 4 3

West	North	East	South
–	–	–	2♣
Pass	2♡	Pass	2♠
Pass	3♣	Pass	3♠
Pass	4♢ (1)	Pass	6♠
All Pass			

(1) A cue bid, with spades agreed; at any rate an encouragement to slam

South saw nothing much to the hand. He won the diamond lead, drew trumps, and played for the clubs to be 2–2. Unlucky.

Do you see the extra chance that he missed? It was the possibility of setting up dummy's hearts. At trick two he should cash ♡ A. He then crosses to ♠ 10, cashes ♡ K, discarding a club, and ruffs a heart. The suit proves to be 4–3, so he ruffs a top diamond, ruffs the last heart good, and draws trumps. The ace of clubs will serve as an entry to the established heart. Should the hearts prove disappointing there will be time to play for a 2–2 break in clubs.

Eliminate the elimination

Back to another hand where the opponents' bidding helps you to place the cards. The line of play originally chosen was fair enough in isolation but it didn't square with East–West's efforts in the auction.

Love all
Dealer South

♠ A K 7 6
♡ 7
♢ J 10 6
♣ Q J 9 7 2

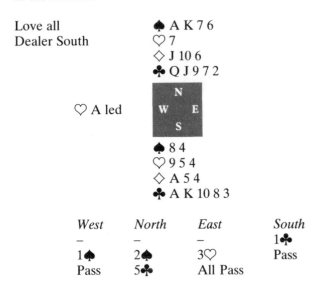

♡ A led

♠ 8 4
♡ 9 5 4
♢ A 5 4
♣ A K 10 8 3

West	North	East	South
–	–	–	1♣
1♠	2♠	3♡	Pass
Pass	5♣	All Pass	

West leads ♡ A and switches to a trump, East following. Does any good plan come to mind?

The original declarer drew a second round of trumps, eliminated the major suits, and played a diamond to the jack. This line would have succeeded if the king and queen of diamonds had been in the same hand. No such luck and he ended one down.

How are the diamond honours likely to lie? West's overcall suggests that he will hold one of them. If he had two, though, he would surely have raised his partner's 3♡ call to game. So, it wouldn't make you fall off your chair to hear that the diamond honours were divided.

So much for the card reading; how can you reap advantage from it? After drawing trumps you should lead a low diamond towards the table. West will doubtless play low, otherwise you would have a subsequent finesse against East's honour. East wins the first diamond and returns, say, another diamond. You rise with the ace, ruff a heart, return to a trump, ruff a heart. When you return to hand with a trump and cash two more rounds of trumps West, with dummy's spades looming over him, will have to find a discard from ♠ Q 10 9 ◇ K. An eleventh trick is on the way.

Back to the bidding

There was a clue in the bidding on this deal too, where the interest lay in how to play the diamond suit.

Love all   ♠ Q 9 2
Dealer East   ♡ 10 7 2
                  ◇ J 8 6 2
                  ♣ A K 5

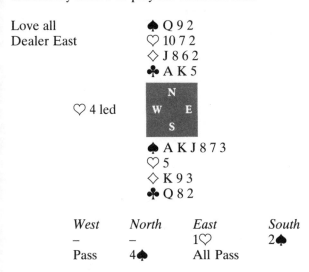

♡ 4 led

♠ A K J 8 7 3
♡ 5
◇ K 9 3
♣ Q 8 2

West	North	East	South
–	–	1♡	2♠
Pass	4♠	All Pass	

East wins the heart lead with the king and continues with the ace of hearts, which you ruff. You draw trumps, finding West with three, and must now decide how to play the diamond suit. Any ideas?

The original declarer could see a clue in the bidding. East had found an opening bid and was therefore likely to hold ◇ A. Yes, a diamond to the king must be right.

A small flaw in this play was exposed when West won with the ace of diamonds and returned another diamond to his partner's Q 10. One down.

East's opening call certainly made it likely that he had one or other diamond honour. Declarer should start with the *jack* of diamonds from the table, intending to run it. If East covers with the queen, the king and ace will complete a heavily-laden trick and the 9 8 will be equals against the 10. And, of course, if West turns up with the diamond queen there will still be time to lead towards the diamond king.

Avoid the guess

On the next deal the opponents maintained a dignified silence during the auction. As a result South faced an eventual guess as to how he should return to hand to draw trumps. It was possible he hadn't chosen the best line in the first place, though. Let's see.

North–South game
Dealer North

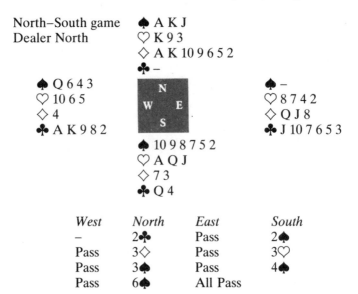

	♠ A K J	
	♡ K 9 3	
	◇ A K 10 9 6 5 2	
	♣ –	
♠ Q 6 4 3		♠ –
♡ 10 6 5		♡ 8 7 4 2
◇ 4		◇ Q J 8
♣ A K 9 8 2		♣ J 10 7 6 5 3
	♠ 10 9 8 7 5 2	
	♡ A Q J	
	◇ 7 3	
	♣ Q 4	

West	North	East	South
–	2♣	Pass	2♠
Pass	3◇	Pass	3♡
Pass	3♠	Pass	4♣
Pass	6♣	All Pass	

West started with a high club, ruffed with the jack, and the ace of trumps then revealed the 4–0 break. Declarer crossed to the jack of hearts and ruffed his remaining club with the spade king. That left this position:

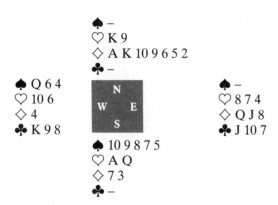

South crossed to the queen of hearts, West dropping a deceptive 10. When he won the next trick with ♠ Q West exited with a diamond to the ace. Declarer now had to guess whether he should return to hand in hearts or by cashing a second diamond and ruffing the third round of diamonds. Deciding to believe West's ♡ 10, he called for the diamond king. Not the best! West ruffed and the slam was one down.

How could declarer have done better? Before crossing to hand to knock out the trump queen he should have cashed the ace of diamonds. In the end position shown, West would then have to provide declarer with a safe route to his hand. Somehow it wasn't easy to see in time that by playing one round of diamonds he would escape the subsequent dilemma.

Brilliancy unrewarded

When you spot a clever line of play it somehow seems all the more annoying if the cards lie adversely and you are robbed of your triumph. That's what happened to declarer on this deal from a teams-of-four match.

North–South game
Dealer South

♠ A 9 4 3
♡ A 2
◇ 9 6 5
♣ J 10 6 3

♠ Q led

```
      N
  W       E
      S
```

♠ –
♡ K 9 8 7 5 3
◇ A K 7 4
♣ A K Q

West	North	East	South
–	–	–	1♡
Pass	1♠	Pass	3◇
Pass	3♡	Pass	4♣
Pass	4♡	Pass	5♣
Pass	6♡	All Pass	

West leads the queen of spades. You have one certain loser in trumps, assuming that they are 3–2; your problem is to avoid a further loser in diamonds.

The original South spotted an imaginative line of play. He ruffed the spade lead, cashed the king of trumps, then played two high clubs from hand. After crossing to dummy with the ace of trumps, he discarded the queen of clubs on the spade ace. He now had two chances of discarding his diamond losers on ♣ J 10: the suit might break 3–3 or the defender with only two clubs might not hold the last trump. These were the defenders' hands, though:

♠ K Q J 6 5   ♠ 10 8 7 2
♡ Q 10 4   ♡ J 6
◇ J 10 8   ◇ Q 3 2
♣ 8 2   ♣ 9 7 5 4

As you see, the applause for declarer's line of play was short-lived; West was able to ruff the third club and the slam went one down.

South was not pleased to find that the slam had been made at the other table. Declarer had cashed the king of trumps and followed with three rounds of clubs from hand. West ruffed the third round but now declarer could win the return, draw the outstanding trump with dummy's ace, and take a discard on ♣ J.

Was this a better line, do you think? It was, because it was slightly more likely that the defender who held two clubs fewer than his partner would have the longer trump holding – three rather than two.

8   The Pressure Game

Many players live through their bridge career without attempting to master squeeze play at all. 'It doesn't often happen', they may say, or 'It's too clever for me'.

Neither of those reflections is well founded. While the procedure may be difficult to comprehend at first, the moment will come when, quite suddenly, the dawn will break. And once you have a general understanding you will see possibilities on innumerable hands.

You probably do know that the object of squeeze play is to force a defender to release one of the guards that he holds. There are two main situations where this may be possible:

(i) when the defender has to discard before the hand which contains the threatening cards,
(ii) when the threatening cards are located in two different hands, declarer's and the dummy.

The so-called 'simple squeeze' comes in either of these forms. This is the first:

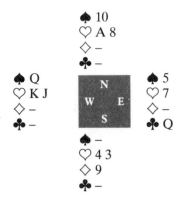

♠ 10
♡ A 8
♢ –
♣ –

♠ Q   ♠ 5
♡ K J   ♡ 7
♢ –   ♢ –
♣ –   ♣ Q

♠ –
♡ 4 3
♢ 9
♣ –

Playing in no-trumps, South leads ♢ 9, the squeeze card. West, who has to discard *before* the dummy, has no good discard. The 'one-card threat' (♠ 10) and the 'two-card threat' (♡ A 8) both lie over him; he is caught in what is known as a one-way, or positional, squeeze.

If you exchanged the East and West cards the squeeze would not work. Declarer would have to throw one of the dummy's threats before East made his critical discard.

It is sometimes possible to squeeze the opponent to the right of the squeeze card, but only if the one-card threat, here ♠ 10, accompanies the squeeze card. This is the second case we noted, where the threat cards are divided between the two hands.

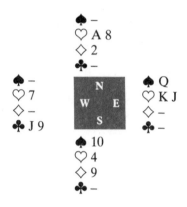

South leads ♢ 9 and East has to abandon one of his guards. This is known as an 'automatic squeeze', since it succeeds whichever defender holds the two guards. You see how the single threat (♠ 10) is more powerful when it accompanies the squeeze card.

Isolating the guard

A threat guarded by only one defender is usually a more powerful asset than one guarded by both defenders. On the next deal declarer ruffs out East's guard in the club suit, so that West will have to bear all the responsibility.

North–South game   ♠ 6
Dealer South   ♡ A 5 2
                       ♢ K 8 7 6 4
                       ♣ K 8 6 4

```
♠ 5 3                              ♠ 9 7 4 2
♡ 10 7          N                  ♡ K 8 6 4 3
♢ J 9 3 2    W     E               ♢ 10
♣ A Q 9 7 2     S                  ♣ 10 5 3
```

                       ♠ A K Q J 10 8
                       ♡ Q J 9
                       ♢ A Q 5
                       ♣ J

West	North	East	South
–	–	–	2♠
Pass	3♢	Pass	4♢
Pass	4♡	Pass	4NT (1)
Pass	5♡ (2)	Pass	6♠
All Pass			

(1) Roman Key-Card Blackwood
(2) Two 'aces' (♡ A and ♢ K, king of the presumed trump suit)

South arrived in six spades and West led the ace of clubs; not a good choice, as it turned out. At trick two he did better. He switched to ♡ 10 and declarer had to go up with the ace, losing what would have been his entry for the fifth diamond.

South made a good play at this point; he cashed the king of clubs and ruffed a club. This essential manoeuvre left West in sole control of the club suit. Declarer then played four rounds of spades, arriving at this position:

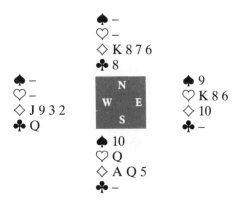

Now the last spade was fatal for West.

Vienna Coup

When we looked at the difference between positional (one-way) and automatic squeezes we saw that a single threat in the same hand as the squeeze card was capable of acting against either opponent. To free a card to do this it is sometimes necessary to cash any winners in the suit held by the opposite hand.

Look at this end position, in which South hopes to make the remaining tricks:

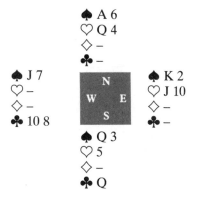

He cashes the queen of clubs, hoping that if the outstanding hearts do not divide someone will be squeezed in the majors. Even though East does hold both major-suit guards the squeeze is not going to work. Declarer will have to find a discard from dummy before East is put to the test; if ♠ 6 is released, East can safely discard his second spade. There will be no entry to South's ♠ Q.

For the squeeze to work, declarer must cash the ace of spades earlier. With no ace of spades, this is the end position:

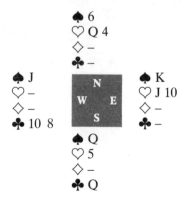

You see the difference? Now when the queen of clubs is led a spade discard from the dummy causes no problem. South's spade queen is free to act as a threat against either player. Here it is East who will go home unhappy.

Let's look at a complete deal involving this idea.

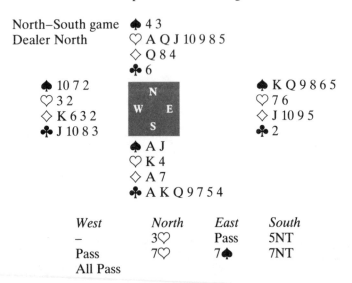

West	North	East	South
–	3♡	Pass	5NT
Pass	7♡	7♠	7NT
All Pass			

South's 5NT asked North to bid the grand slam if he held two of the top three heart honours. After this confident auction East was sure that the heart grand would succeed. He sacrificed in seven spades, knowing that he could afford to go a great number down and still show a profit. South was not to be denied, though; indeed he may have intended to bid 7NT in any event.

West led a low spade, which ran to the queen and ace. Now South made an excellent play: he cashed the ace of diamonds (Vienna Coup), freeing dummy's queen to act as a menace against either opponent. Next came six rounds of hearts, to leave this position:

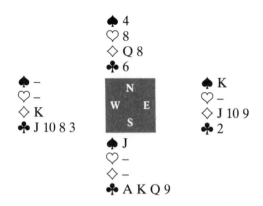

```
            ♠ 4
            ♡ 8
            ◇ Q 8
            ♣ 6
♠ -                      ♠ K
♡ -                      ♡ -
◇ K                      ◇ J 10 9
♣ J 10 8 3               ♣ 2
            ♠ J
            ♡ -
            ◇ -
            ♣ A K Q 9
```

On the last heart South discarded the jack of spades and West was squeezed. It couldn't have been done if South had retained the ace of diamonds; this card would have blocked the diamond suit in the event of West baring the king of diamonds when the last heart was played.

What did you think of West's spade lead? Not brilliant. He could be fairly certain that South's suit was clubs, and leading ♣ J would have spoiled declarer's entries. But what should South do if a club is led? His best chance would be to cash three clubs, ◇ A, then dummy's heart suit. This line would succeed if East held ◇ K and ♠ K Q.

Double squeeze

A double squeeze, in which both opponents are involved, is not uncommon. A superhuman diamond lead would have defeated

South's contract on this deal, but West's fingers alighted on the king of hearts.

Love all
Dealer South

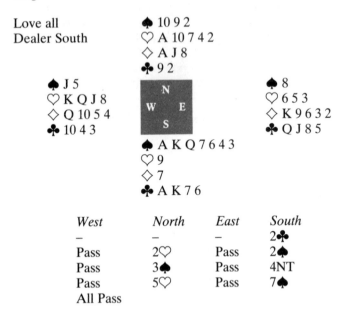

♠ 10 9 2
♡ A 10 7 4 2
♢ A J 8
♣ 9 2

♠ J 5
♡ K Q J 8
♢ Q 10 5 4
♣ 10 4 3

♠ 8
♡ 6 5 3
♢ K 9 6 3 2
♣ Q J 8 5

♠ A K Q 7 6 4 3
♡ 9
♢ 7
♣ A K 7 6

West	North	East	South
–	–	–	2♣
Pass	2♡	Pass	2♠
Pass	3♠	Pass	4NT
Pass	5♡	Pass	7♠
All Pass			

South was the sort of player who liked to make the most of any good hand that came his way. He soared into seven spades, undeterred by the possibility of a loser or two in clubs.

The heart lead was won in the dummy and declarer ruffed a heart immediately, since there was some chance that he might be able to establish a long heart. West dropped the jack on this trick, in the faint hope that this would cause declarer to place him with K Q J alone.

Both defenders followed to the ace of spades but the jack did not drop. South might have tried to ruff two clubs now, but there were other chances. He cashed a second spade, ruffed the third round of clubs, and ruffed another heart. Both defenders followed to this trick, but there were insufficient entries to make anything of the fifth heart. South decided to run his spade suit and this ending resulted:

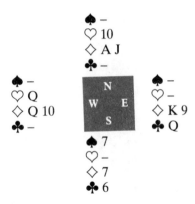

On the last trump West had to throw a diamond, to retain his guard against dummy's ♡ 10. This card could now be spared from the table, leaving East to give way in one or other minor suit.

You would summarize the play in this way: West had to guard the hearts, East had to guard the clubs; neither defender could therefore guard the diamond suit.

A question of timing

A general rule in squeeze play is that if you are in, say, 3NT, and can see eight tricks on top but no obvious chance of a ninth, you should aim to lose four tricks quite early on. By achieving the desired position of being able to win 'all the remaining tricks but one', you tighten the end position and remove the defenders' surplus cards. By *rectifying the count*, as it is called, you greatly increase the chances that one of other defender will be ripe for a squeeze.

With this piece of advice before you, you should be able to solve the small problem on this deal:

Love all
Dealer West

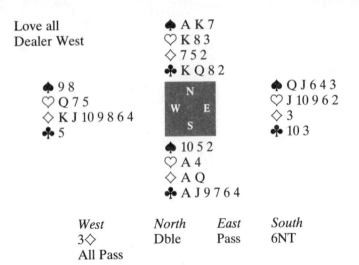

```
                    ♠ A K 7
                    ♡ K 8 3
                    ◇ 7 5 2
                    ♣ K Q 8 2
  ♠ 9 8                              ♠ Q J 6 4 3
  ♡ Q 7 5              N             ♡ J 10 9 6 2
  ◇ K J 10 9 8 6 4   W   E          ◇ 3
  ♣ 5                  S             ♣ 10 3
                    ♠ 10 5 2
                    ♡ A 4
                    ◇ A Q
                    ♣ A J 9 7 6 4
```

West	North	East	South
West	*North*	*East*	*South*
3◇	Dble	Pass	6NT
All Pass			

West led ♠ 9 and dummy went up with the ace. What now? There are eleven tricks on top, but not much prospect of a throw-in to score the twelfth. (West will unblock or discard his ♡ Q to avoid being thrown in.)

The best line is to play for a squeeze. South's ♠ 10 is surely a threat against East; and if a diamond is surrendered, the third diamond in dummy will be a threat against West. So, at trick two you rectify the count (remember that phrase?) by leading a diamond to the queen. Some partners would think you hadn't heard the bidding.

West wins and will probably lead his second spade. You win and play for this ending:

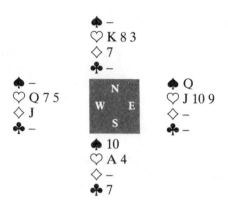

It is another example of the double squeeze. South's ♣ 7 extracts a heart from each defender in turn.

Early claim

Most of the hands in this chapter have contained long suits on both sides of the table. It is not always like that, but such hands take less time to describe and it is easier to concentrate on the end position. This time, everyone has a long suit except for North, who is the calm in the centre of the storm.

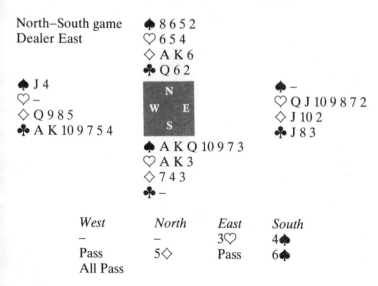

North–South game
Dealer East

West	North	East	South
–	–	3♡	4♠
Pass	5◇	Pass	6♠
All Pass			

117

North's five diamonds was clearly a control in this sequence, implying useful support for South's spades. West led ♣ K, the standard lead against a high contract even if you normally lead the ace; you expect partner to give you a length signal (low from an odd number, high from an even number) letting you know if the other honour will stand up. Here the signal was irrelevant, South ruffing the first trick.

After drawing trumps the declarer consulted his ancestors and finally ducked a round of hearts. His plan was to squeeze West if this player held five diamonds as well as the presumed ace of clubs. The scheme failed because in the end-game East was able to guard the diamonds, allowing West to retain a club guard.

South was too late in forming his plan. He could see eleven tricks on top and the very first trick would not have been too soon to prepare for a squeeze. Instead of ruffing ♣ A he should have discarded a diamond, a play that would have done no injury to his various threat cards.

West would probably switch to a trump and this would be the position after six rounds of spades:

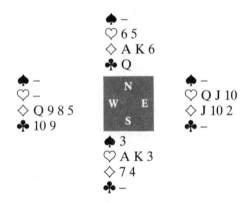

On the last spade West discards a diamond, North a club, and East (in order to retain his heart guard) a diamond. Now the ace and king of hearts put West to the sword.

It was good play on general principles to discard on the opening club lead, but did it occur to you that the exact ending could have been foreseen the moment dummy went down? The diamond discard by declarer was bound to lead to a squeeze.

Since West was marked with ♣ A and East with the long hearts neither would be able to guard the diamond suit.

Declarer might even have claimed the contract at trick one, making his local reputation at least.

The trump squeeze

In a trump contract you have another possible threat against the defenders, that of ruffing a suit good. The extra power is shown by this deal:

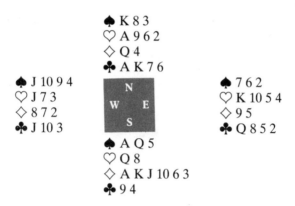

Imagine first that you are in 7NT, West leading the jack of spades. There are twelve tricks on top but chances of a thirteenth are remote. You would have to cash the ace of hearts (Vienna Coup) and play off your winners in spades and diamonds. You would succeed only if a defender had ♡ K and *five* clubs, giving him sole control of those two suits.

Seven diamonds, provided you escape a heart lead, is a better contract; you have the additional chance of ruffing the third round of clubs and so establishing the fourth club as a threat card. If West held ♡ K and four clubs it would be easy to set up a positional squeeze against him. The interesting question is . . . can East be squeezed if he holds both guards?

Suppose you cash the spades and all the trumps except two. This will be the end position:

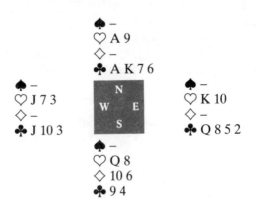

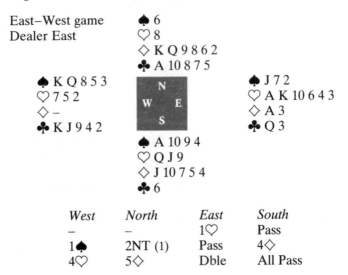

On the penultimate trump you throw ♡ 9 from dummy. East now has no good discard. If he throws a club you can ruff the suit good, reaching the long card via ♡ A. If instead he bares the ♡ K, you cross to ♡ A and eventually return to the South hand with a club ruff to score ♡ Q. You must read the situation correctly, it's true. That's often the case with trump squeezes, as they are called.

Another situation where the trump suit may make its effect felt is when declarer has two long side suits, either one of which might be established by ruffing.

West	North	East	South
–	–	1♡	Pass
1♠	2NT (1)	Pass	4◇
4♡	5◇	Dble	All Pass

(1) Unusual No-trump, showing the two lowest unbid suits

120

Eleven tricks would have been available on a cross-ruff but the defenders prevent this by a lead to ♡ K, followed by ace and another trump. If clubs divide 4–3 there will be no problem; you have enough trumps left in the South hand to ruff dummy's clubs good. Now for a less convenient distribution, West holding five clubs. Since East did not raise spades West's likely shape is 5–3–0–5. Having already discarded a spade and a heart on the trump leads, he will be embarrassed by your second heart ruff.

So, win the second trump in hand, ruff a heart, then play ♣ A and return to hand with a club ruff. These cards will remain:

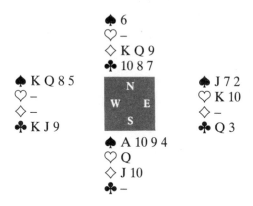

This is the critical moment. You lead ♡ Q and West must weaken his holding in one or other black suit. You will be able to ruff a card good in whichever suit he discards. Had you ruffed a club or two prematurely, playing for a 4–3 club break, West would subsequently have had a safe discard in spades. There would no longer be sufficient entries to establish and enjoy a long spade in the South hand.

Squeeze without the count

In most squeezes it suits declarer to tighten the end position by losing, early on, the tricks he can afford to lose. Sometimes this is not possible; if declarer ducks an early trick the opponents may be able to make some damaging play immediately. Nor is it always essential; declarer may be able to exert pressure by running his long suit, subsequently conceding a trick to the opponents.

We have moved into the kingdom of the 'squeeze without the count'. These occur quite frequently and have perhaps not received the attention from bridge writers that they deserve. See what happens to poor West on this deal:

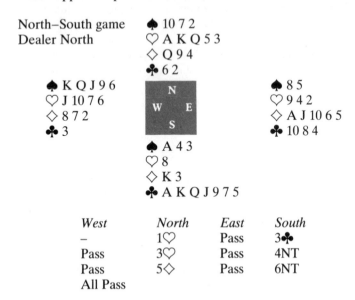

North–South game
Dealer North

```
                    ♠ 10 7 2
                    ♡ A K Q 5 3
                    ◇ Q 9 4
                    ♣ 6 2
♠ K Q J 9 6                         ♠ 8 5
♡ J 10 7 6          N              ♡ 9 4 2
◇ 8 7 2          W     E           ◇ A J 10 6 5
♣ 3                 S              ♣ 10 8 4
                    ♠ A 4 3
                    ♡ 8
                    ◇ K 3
                    ♣ A K Q J 9 7 5
```

West	North	East	South
–	1♡	Pass	3♣
Pass	3♡	Pass	4NT
Pass	5◇	Pass	6NT
All Pass			

Six clubs would have been easy, since declarer can discard his two spade losers on the hearts and set up a twelfth trick in diamonds. Hoping to make up lost ground in a pairs tournament, though, South on this deal took a somewhat wild path to 6NT.

The king of spades was led and it was extremely dangerous to duck this card (to rectify the count) because the defenders might then cash the ace of diamonds. South won the first trick with the spade ace and, with nothing else to try, put the defenders to the ordeal by running the club suit. This was the position with one club still to be played:

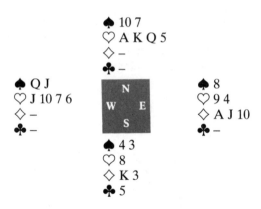

West had to keep four hearts to guard against the dummy's holding. It made no difference at this stage whether he had kept two good spades alongside, or a spade and a diamond. Either way, when the last club was led West had to reduce to one good spade and his four hearts. It was not difficult for declarer to read the position. He threw a heart from the table and led a spade, setting up dummy's ♠ 10 as the twelfth trick.

The play is known as a 'squeeze without the count', since the count had not been rectified at the moment the squeeze occurred. Declarer lost a trick *after* West had been squeezed.

Sometimes the defender who is overloaded with high cards must concede even more ground. Not only is he forced to discard winners, he is then thrown in to concede a trick elsewhere. Hands such as the following are quite common.

East–West game
Dealer West

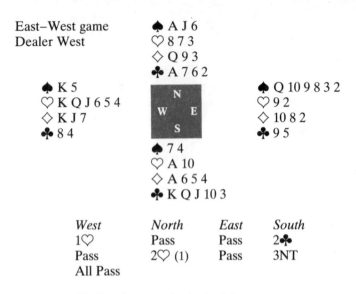

	♠ A J 6		
	♡ 8 7 3		
	◊ Q 9 3		
	♣ A 7 6 2		

♠ K 5   ♠ Q 10 9 8 3 2
♡ K Q J 6 5 4   ♡ 9 2
◊ K J 7   ◊ 10 8 2
♣ 8 4   ♣ 9 5

♠ 7 4
♡ A 10
◊ A 6 5 4
♣ K Q J 10 3

West	*North*	*East*	*South*
1♡	Pass	Pass	2♣
Pass	2♡ (1)	Pass	3NT
All Pass			

(1) Showing a good raise in clubs

South could hardly be better for his two-club overcall in the protective position, since with a sixth club he would have been worth an intermediate three-club overcall. He therefore goes all the way to 3NT when his partner makes an enthusiastic move.

Take over South's hand now. How would you react after the lead of the king of hearts? There are only eight tricks on top and little would be gained by holding up the ace of hearts. For one thing, a spade switch would be unwelcome; also by capturing immediately you retain the option of later throwing West in with ♡ 10.

You win the first heart and run the club suit. West abandons his spade holding, which was valueless under dummy's A J, and this position is reached:

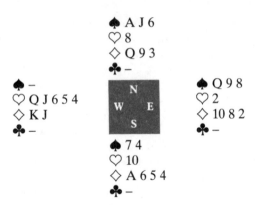

```
              ♠ A J 6
              ♡ 8
              ◇ Q 9 3
              ♣ -
♠ -                          ♠ Q 9 8
♡ Q J 6 5 4      N           ♡ 2
◇ K J        W     E         ◇ 10 8 2
♣ -              S           ♣ -
              ♠ 7 4
              ♡ 10
              ◇ A 6 5 4
              ♣ -
```

A spade to the ace has West on the ropes. If he bares the diamond king you will score two tricks in that suit; if instead he throws a heart, you will exit in hearts and West will have to lead from ◇ K at trick 12.

The next deal was unusual because the throw-in occurred in a suit where the defender had what looks to be an almost solid holding.

Love all
Dealer South

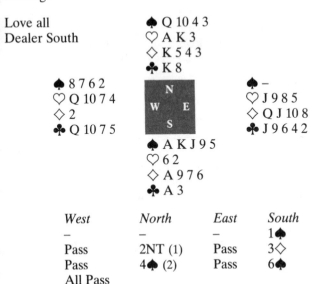

```
                  ♠ Q 10 4 3
                  ♡ A K 3
                  ◇ K 5 4 3
                  ♣ K 8
♠ 8 7 6 2                        ♠ -
♡ Q 10 7 4      N                ♡ J 9 8 5
◇ 2          W     E             ◇ Q J 10 8
♣ Q 10 7 5      S                ♣ J 9 6 4 2
                  ♠ A K J 9 5
                  ♡ 6 2
                  ◇ A 9 7 6
                  ♣ A 3
```

West	North	East	South
–	–	–	1♠
Pass	2NT (1)	Pass	3◇
Pass	4♠ (2)	Pass	6♠
All Pass			

(1) Baron 2NT, flat hand of around 16 points upwards
(2) Lower-range Baron bid, four-card trump support

West leads ♢ 2 and East attempts to muddy the waters by contributing the jack, won by the ace. Despite East's antics declarer is inclined to place West with the singleton diamond. Apart from the fact that West would scarcely lead from length into a bid suit, the slam cannot be made if East's ♢ J was a singleton.

If trumps were not 4–0, declarer could make the hand on an elimination (draw trumps, eliminate hearts and clubs, and play a diamond to the 9). The bad trump break makes life awkward, though, and South turns his mind to an eventual throw-in against East.

Before this can happen East must be squeezed out of his safe exit cards. Declarer therefore plays off five rounds of trumps, East throwing three hearts and two clubs. After the ace of clubs and a top heart have been cashed these cards remain:

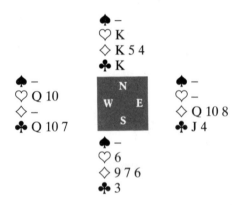

To cash ♣ K would cost the contract. Since East has already played four hearts, though, it is unlikely that he has two more remaining. Declarer therefore cashes ♡ K, squeezing a reluctant club from East. The king of clubs now draws East's last card outside diamonds and a diamond to the 9 finishes the matter.

As you see, it was important to cash the ace of clubs first, rather than the king. Declarer needed to be in dummy to effect the throw-in.

The repeating squeeze

All the squeezes we have seen until now have yielded only one trick. Occasionally a defender holds the sole guard in three suits. You may be able to squeeze him out of one of his guards, then play the established winner in that suit to squeeze him again. It wasn't difficult on this deal because West's intervention in the auction told declarer how the cards lay.

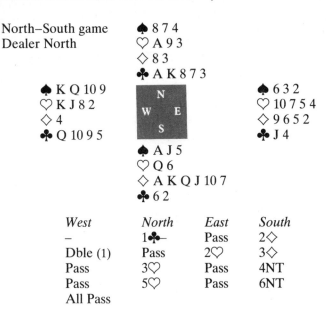

North–South game
Dealer North

♠ 8 7 4
♡ A 9 3
◇ 8 3
♣ A K 8 7 3

♠ K Q 10 9
♡ K J 8 2
◇ 4
♣ Q 10 9 5

♠ 6 3 2
♡ 10 7 5 4
◇ 9 6 5 2
♣ J 4

♠ A J 5
♡ Q 6
◇ A K Q J 10 7
♣ 6 2

West	North	East	South
–	1♣–	Pass	2◇
Dble (1)	Pass	2♡	3◇
Pass	3♡	Pass	4NT
Pass	5♡	Pass	6NT
All Pass			

(1) A ridiculous move when he knows that the opponents have all the other good cards. How often do you see such calls made, though?

Six diamonds would have been a more flexible contract, with the additional chance of ruffing the clubs good. However, it was a pairs tournament and South took a flier at 6NT.

West led ♠ K, East discouraging with the 2 and declarer holding off ♠ A. When West switched to a diamond declarer won in the South hand, cashed dummy's ♡ A (a Vienna Coup to free his queen), and ran the diamond suit. He had only ten tricks on top and needed to score two more from this squeeze ending:

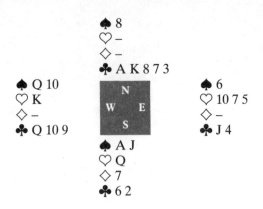

```
              ♠ 8
              ♡ –
              ◇ –
              ♣ A K 8 7 3
♠ Q 10                        ♠ 6
♡ K        ┌──────────┐       ♡ 10 7 5
◇ –        │    N     │       ◇ –
♣ Q 10 9   │ W      E │       ♣ J 4
           │    S     │
           └──────────┘
              ♠ A J
              ♡ Q
              ◇ 7
              ♣ 6 2
```

What could West throw on the last diamond? A club would immediately surrender two tricks. If he threw a heart or a spade, declarer would cash the established winner in that suit to squeeze West again. It looked as if declarer had been really clever but in fact there was nothing much to it, except for remembering to cash the ace of hearts before running the diamonds.

Still, that didn't prevent South from telling every bridge player he met for the next few months about his wonderful play. There are many qualities you need to reach the top at bridge. Modesty is not one of them.